ASIA

EUROPE

Antwerp

Genoa   Venice

Barcelona

Tordesillas   Naples

SPAIN

Seville

Lisbon

Sagres   Granada

Palos

PORTUGAL

AZORES ISLANDS

COLUMBUS 1492-1493
(1st voyage)

CANARY
ISLANDS

MOROCCO

Cape Bojador

Cape Blanco

MEDITERRANEAN SEA

Rhodes

TURKEY

Carthage   Alexandria

Cairo

Mt.
Ararat

CASPIAN SEA

PAMIR
MTS.

PERSIA

PERSIAN
GULF   Hormuz

INDIA

Cambay

SAHARA

EGYPT

RED SEA

Mecca

ARABIAN
SEA   Goa

BAHAMA ISLANDS
Watlings Island

SARGASSO
SEA

CUBA

Navidad
Jamaica   Hispaniola   Puerto Rico

LEEWARD ISLANDS

HONDURAS

PANAMA
DARIEN

Trinidad   MOUTH OF
THE ORINOCO R.

CAPE VERDE
ISLANDS

Cape Verde

SIERRA
LEONE

GOLD
COAST

Lagos

NIGERIA   AFRICA

ETHIOPIA

Malabar Coast

Calicut
Cochin

CEYLON

R. Niger

GULF OF GUINEA

Mt. Cameroon

KENYA

SOMALIA

INDIAN OCEAN

ATLANTIC OCEAN

Cape
Santa Catarina

River Amazon

Natal

Recife

SOUTH
AMERICA   BRAZIL

R. Congo

DIAS
1487-1488

ANGOLA

Malindi
Mombasa

Kilwa

Equator

Mozambique

MADAGASCAR

Sofala

CABRAL 1500-1501

DA GAMA 1497-1499

Rio de Janeiro

Cape Cross

WALVIS BAY

Lüderitz
Orange River

NATAL

ARGENTINA

Montevideo

RIO DE LA PLATA

ST. HELENA BAY

Cape of
Good Hope

Keiskama Point
Kwaaihoek

ALGOA BAY

RIO DOS VAQUEIROS

Cape Agulhas

CHILE
PATAGONIA

BAHIA DE LOS PATOS

Port St. Julian
Puerto Santa Cruz.

Cape of
Desire   Cape of the Virgins

STRAIT OF MAGELLAN

The Seafarers THE EXPLORERS

The Cover: In a frantic attempt to escape
predators, schools of flying fish sail into the
rigging of a Portuguese vessel off the
coast of Brazil in the 16th Century. Though
artist Theodore de Bry never went on
such a voyage himself, he noted with care
the explorers' descriptions in order to
render this finny phenomenon accurately.

The Title Page: Hand painted in high
relief in 1515, this nine-and-one-half-inch
wooden *Globe Vert*—called the "Green
Globe" because of the brilliant color of its
seas—shows with considerable
accuracy the discoveries of southern
regions of the African continent.

THE EXPLORERS

by Richard Humble

AND THE EDITORS OF TIME-LIFE BOOKS

TIME-LIFE BOOKS, ALEXANDRIA, VIRGINIA

Time-Life Books Inc.
is a wholly owned subsidiary of
TIME INCORPORATED

FOUNDER: Henry R. Luce 1898-1967

Editor-in-Chief: Hedley Donovan
Chairman of the Board: Andrew Heiskell
President: James R. Shepley
Vice Chairmen: Roy E. Larsen, Arthur Temple
Corporate Editors: Ralph Graves,
Henry Anatole Grunwald

TIME-LIFE BOOKS INC.

MANAGING EDITOR: Jerry Korn
Executive Editor: David Maness
Assistant Managing Editors: Dale M. Brown (planning),
George Constable, Jim Hicks (acting), Martin Mann,
John Paul Porter
Art Director: Tom Suzuki
Chief of Research: David L. Harrison
Director of Photography: Robert G. Mason
Senior Text Editor: Diana Hirsh
Assistant Art Director: Arnold C. Holeywell
Assistant Chief of Research: Carolyn L. Sackett
Assistant Director of Photography: Dolores A. Littles

CHAIRMAN: Joan D. Manley
President: John D. McSweeney
Executive Vice Presidents: Carl G. Jaeger,
John Steven Maxwell, David J. Walsh
Vice Presidents: Peter G. Barnes (comptroller),
Nicholas Benton (public relations), John L. Canova (sales),
Nicholas J. C. Ingleton (Asia), James L. Mercer
(Europe/South Pacific), Herbert Sorkin (production),
Paul R. Stewart (promotion)
Personnel Director: Beatrice T. Dobie
Consumer Affairs Director: Carol Flaumenhaft

The Seafarers

Editorial Staff for The Explorers:
Editor: George G. Daniels
Designer: Herbert H. Quarmby
Text Editors: Anne Horan, Sterling Seagrave
Staff Writers: Susan Bryan, Gus Hedberg
Chief Researcher: Martha T. Goolrick
Researchers: William C. Banks, Regina Cahill,
Charlie Clark, Jane Coughran, Philip George,
W. Mark Hamilton, Katie Hooper McGregor,
Peggy L. Sawyer, Nancy Toff
Art Assistants: Santi José Acosta, Michelle Clay
Editorial Assistant: Feroline Burrage

Editorial Production
Production Editor: Douglas B. Graham
Operations Manager: Gennaro C. Esposito,
Gordon E. Buck (assistant)
Assistant Production Editor: Feliciano Madrid
Quality Control: Robert L. Young (director), James J. Cox
(assistant), Michael G. Wight (associate)
Art Coordinator: Anne B. Landry
Copy Staff: Susan B. Galloway (chief), Sheirazada Hann,
Elise D. Ritter, Celia Beattie
Picture Department: Marguerite Johnson
Traffic: Jeanne Potter

Correspondents: Elisabeth Kraemer (Bonn); Margot
Hapgood, Dorothy Bacon (London); Susan Jonas, Lucy
T. Voulgaris (New York); Maria Vincenza Aloisi,
Josephine du Brusle (Paris); Ann Natanson (Rome).
Valuable assistance was also provided by: Janny
Hovinga (Amsterdam); Nina Lindley (Buenos Aires); Ole
Schierbeck (Copenhagen); Peter Hawthorne
(Johannesburg); Tomas Loayza (Lima); Martha de la Cal
(Lisbon); Penny Newman (London); Bill Lyon (Madrid);
Benjamin Defensor (Manila); Bernard Diederich (Mexico
City); Carolyn T. Chubet, Miriam Hsia (New York);
Alison Raphael (Rio de Janeiro); Mimi Murphy (Rome).

The editors are indebted to Barbara Hicks, Wendy Buehr
Murphy, Richard Seamon and David Thomson for their
help in the preparation of this book.

The Author:
Richard Humble, a biographer and historian, was educated at Oriel College, Oxford, specializing in military history. The author of Captain Bligh, a reappraisal of the much-maligned commander of the H.M.S. Bounty, he has also written Marco Polo, Hitler's Generals and Before the Dreadnought.

The Consultants:
John Horace Parry, Gardiner Professor of Oceanic History and Affairs at Harvard University, was educated at Clare College, Cambridge University, where he took his Ph.D. He served in the Royal Navy during World War II, rising to the rank of commander. He is the author of 10 books, including The Discovery of the Sea, The Spanish Seaborne Empire, Europe and a Wider World and Trade and Dominion.

William Avery Baker, a naval architect and engineer, is curator of the Hart Nautical Museum at the Massachusetts Institute of Technology, where he took his degree. He designed and supervised construction of a number of 17th and 18th Century sailing craft, including the Mayflower II, which sailed from England to Plymouth, Massachusetts, in 1957.

Library of Congress Cataloging in Publication Data
Humble, Richard
   The Explorers
   (The seafarers; v. 3)
   Bibliography: p.
   Includes index.
   1. Explorers. I. Time-Life Books.
II. Title. III. Series.
G200.H85   910',92'2[B]   78-1292
ISBN 0-8094-2660-9
ISBN 0-8094-2659-5 lib. bdg.

Contents

Man's ever-enlarging view of his planet

In 14th Century Europe, just before the dawn of the great age of discovery, ordinary men believed that beyond the reaches of the known world lay nothing but chaos and an infinite abyss. They imagined that the sky did not envelop the whole earth but covered only the top, while the bottom was somehow anchored to something. They thought that the stars moved, while earth and sky remained stationary. And they believed that if people inhabited the earth's nether regions, they must walk with feet up and heads down.

Some medieval scholars, those with access to the hidden knowledge of antiquity, recognized these fantasies for what they were. But there was no way to prove them false. Mariners would not venture much beyond their coasts. Only a short distance from the Strait of Gibraltar, they said, lay a vast, entrapping Sea of Mud resulting from the sinking of the legendary city of Atlantis.

Then, suddenly, at the close of the 15th and the beginning of the 16th centuries, all of the wild imaginings and murky half-logic were swept away. Driven by a thirst for power, glory and wealth, a handful of courageous and determined explorers—Bartolomeu Dias, Vasco da Gama, Christopher Columbus, Ferdinand Magellan and a few others—journeyed forth to conquer the unknown.

The ships they sailed were unhandy. Their navigational instruments were crude and their maps—both academic ones, such as the 13th Century theological *Mappa Mundi* at right, and working charts—reflected the Christian world's ignorance after a millennium in the Dark Ages.

Even the best of these first maps were artful blends of scant information and much guesswork. The faraway landfalls they described in Asia were constructed from the tales of medieval missionaries and traders who ranged eastward during the time when the Great Khan of Cathay still tolerated visitors from strange lands. This parade of itinerant merchants and friars had made the long journey to Malaya and Malabar, and to China. It did not matter whether the stories brought home were the careful reports of Marco Polo or the fraudulent fantasies of dreamers, all of them had an impact on the cartographer's art.

For hundreds of years, as traders coasted along the Mediterranean littoral, pilots had recorded routes and distances from port to port, the look of the land and the way the winds blew. Written sailing directions and the charts of that small part of the world were relatively reliable guides. Coastlines were sketched in with reasonable accuracy, compass roses showing directions were provided, and rhumb lines of constant bearing made a network to aid the navigator. But when the great voyagers shaped their courses south and west from Portugal's Cape St. Vincent, they had no such aids. The rudimentary charts they carried described their goals only in the sketchiest fashion.

The sophisticated calculations of Ptolemy, the Second Century geographer who had recognized the problems of projecting the surface of a sphere on a flat map, and the inspired mathematics of Eratosthenes, who had measured the globe with remarkable accuracy more than a thousand years before, had only recently been rediscovered. But those intellectual achievements were not yet fully appreciated nor understood by 15th Century cartographers.

So the explorers of the time became, in effect, scientists. With their bold experiments they tested theory in the harsh laboratory of practice. They gambled their lives on finding new lands, new ocean passages, and to their everlasting glory they succeeded. Of all the treasure they brought home from those short decades of astonishing adventure, none exceeded in importance their hard-won knowledge, the observations and experiences that taught man at last the true shape and size of his world.

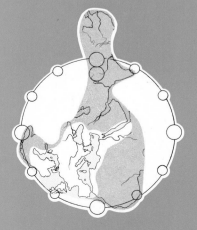

Taken from a 13th Century English Psalter, this "wheel map" (right) is more reflective of a state of mind than useful as an aid to navigation. With Biblical orthodoxy, Jerusalem stands at the hub of the world; the Garden of Eden is to the east (at top); and Europe lies to the northwest (at bottom left). The diagram at left and those on the next pages indicate on modern Mercator's projections the limits of the early mapmakers' world. In this case, with Jerusalem at the center and east at the top, the salient features of the ancient wheel map (shown in white) include most of Europe, the Mediterranean and virtually all of the Red Sea. But most of Africa and Asia (shaded areas) were unknown.

8

The wonderful calculations of Claudius Ptolemaeus

Overlaid on the modern map at bottom, the Second Century A.D. world of Claudius Ptolemaeus, better known as Ptolemy, is only a fraction of its true size. Most of Africa and Asia remain to be explored; the New World is as yet undreamed of. And what is known is warped by wide distortions.

In this 15th Century chart, based on Ptolemy's *Geography*, the Mediterranean is drawn with some precision; Europe, too, and parts of Asia are easily recognizable. But beyond familiar trade routes, land masses take on odd shapes. The seas are confined or vastly exaggerated. A single continent, the Terra Incognita of the antipodes, extends across the bottom of the world. Africa is broader than life, chopped off and flattened to the south, leaving the Indian Ocean landlocked. Africa's interior is more accurate, but Asia reflects the mistakes and colorful lies of early travelers.

Despite errors, Ptolemy's geography gave 15th Century mapmakers a system of coordinates for making reliable sea charts. He divided the globe into the now-standard 360°, devised a formula to describe how the length of a degree of longitude changes with latitude changes and attempted to project the curved earth onto flat maps.

Though the locations Ptolemy recorded were often out of kilter, the calculations he made marked the beginning of scientific cartography.

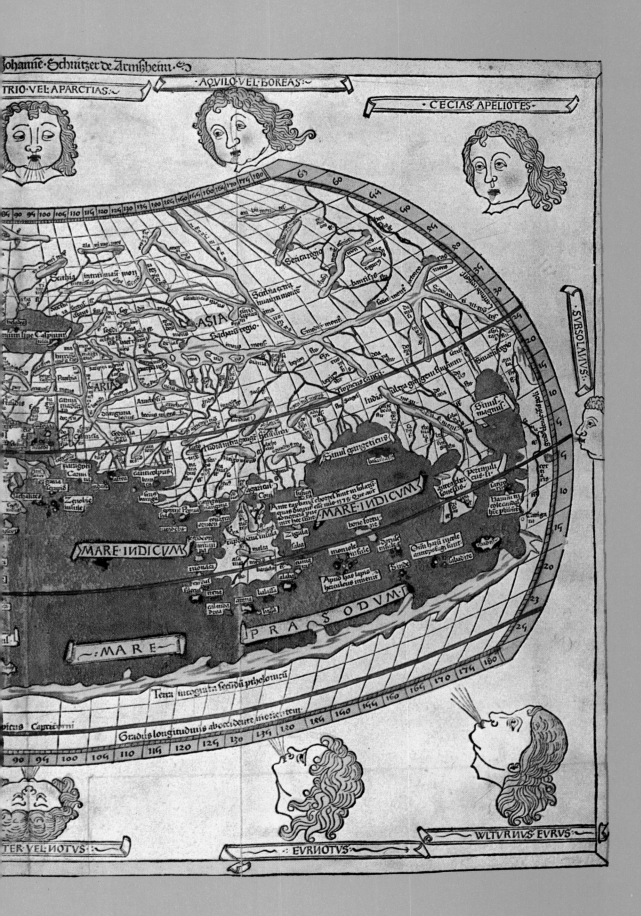

A geography devised by mariners

Once Ptolemy's theories and measurements were resurrected, cartographers tended to think of them as unassailable. The explorers, on the other hand, showed no such reluctance to challenge accepted authority. They had no patience with scholarly argument. Errors cost lives. Once found, mistakes on maps had to be corrected lest dangers be revisited on other sailors.

This Ptolemaic map drawn by German cartographer Henricus Martellus in about 1490 reflects the discoveries made by Bartolomeu Dias and other explorers up to that time. As can be seen on the diagram at bottom, the known world has expanded widely.

Now the land bridge between southern Africa and southeast Asia—which earlier cartographers included on their maps—has been discarded. "The true modern form of Africa from the description of the Portuguese" is the proud label on the Dark Continent. All along the coast, place names mark Dias' progress.

Once Dias doubled the Cape of Good Hope, the actual shape of the African shore began to show up on charts. But while Martellus' map shows that an eastward passage around Africa is possible, it also correctly shows it to be a long and arduous voyage. This was the geography Columbus would count on a few years later—for by inference, the unseen backside of Martellus' world was empty ocean, affording a swift and unhindered route west to the Orient.

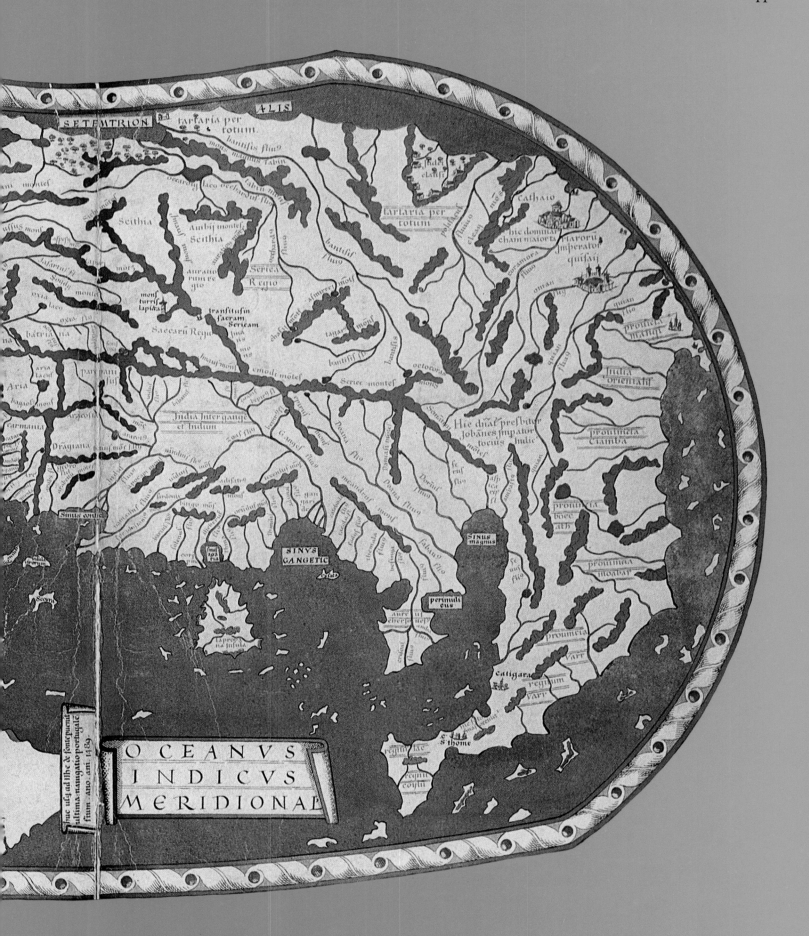

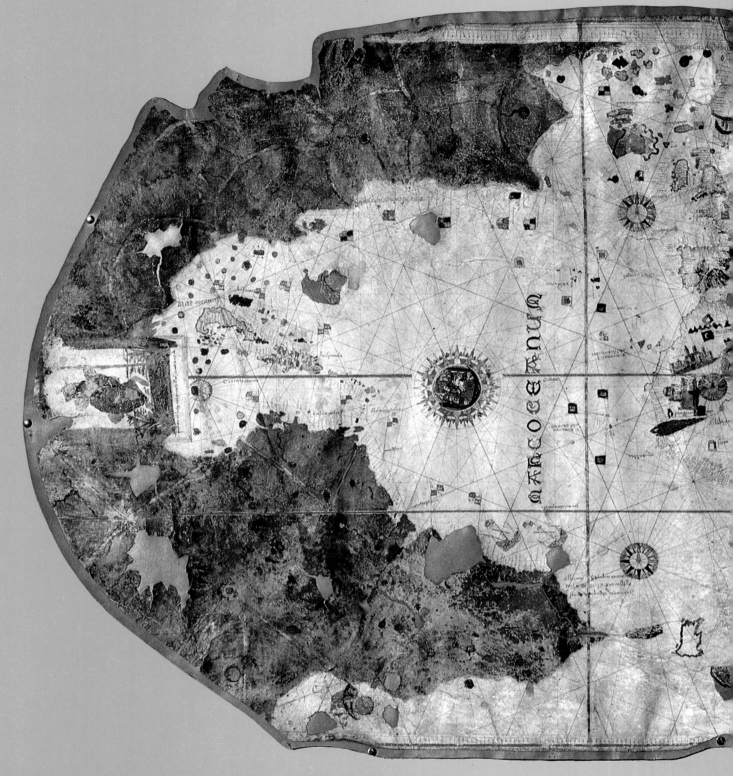

Sailing directions across a watery void

Artfully drawn to aid ocean navigators, this chart, probably by Juan de la Cosa, one of Columbus' officers, must have seemed invaluable to explorers of the early 16th Century. The weblike network of lines reaching from edge to edge is composed of rhumb lines —direct courses of constant bearing from one point to another. If the chartmaker was unaware that his calculations could become seriously distorted when extended across thousands of miles of ocean, he was nonetheless careful to include on his chart the latest knowledge carried back home by adventurous mariners.

As indicated on the diagram at right, the coasts of both Africa and India are at this time known to mariners, and both North and South America are beginning to show up on charts. There are still great distortions on de la Co-

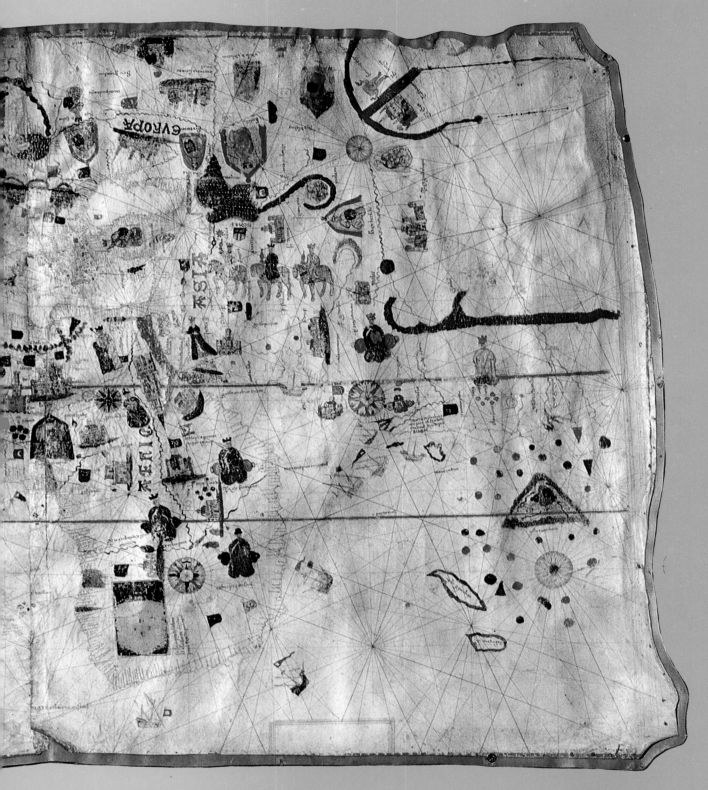

sa's map. But he takes care to correct one of Columbus' errors. Obsessed with the idea that he had sailed to the Orient, Columbus insisted that Cuba was part of the mainland. However, de la Cosa apparently knew better in 1500 when he drew this chart. Cuba, which was not circumnavigated until 1508, is shown here as an island.

14

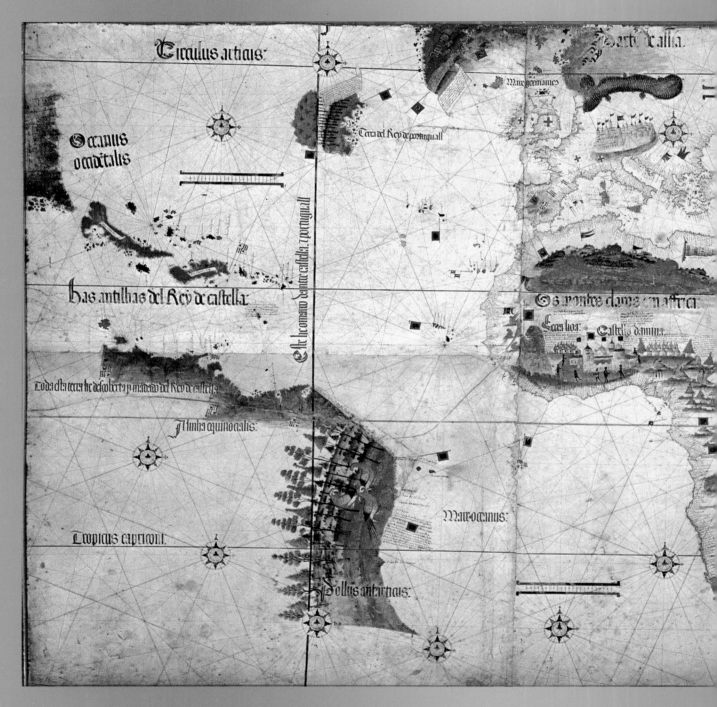

Portugal's jealously guarded exploration routes

From the logs of more and more voyages, the shape of the West Indies and South America began to evolve with increasing accuracy. João II of Portugal had good reason to forbid any foreigner access to his country's charts. They were, after all, the key to trade and treasure. In 1502, an Italian secret agent, Alberto Cantino, had to pay 12 gold ducats to commission this illegal copy of the official Portuguese *padron,* the world map on which all new discoveries were recorded. The prize he brought to his employer, the Duke of Ferrara, was worth the price.

Cantino's smuggled chart extends across 257° of longitude; the remaining 103°, as can be seen on the diagram at right, had yet to be explored by a European mariner. It seems clear, though, that the mapmaker admitted the possibility that the Americas were

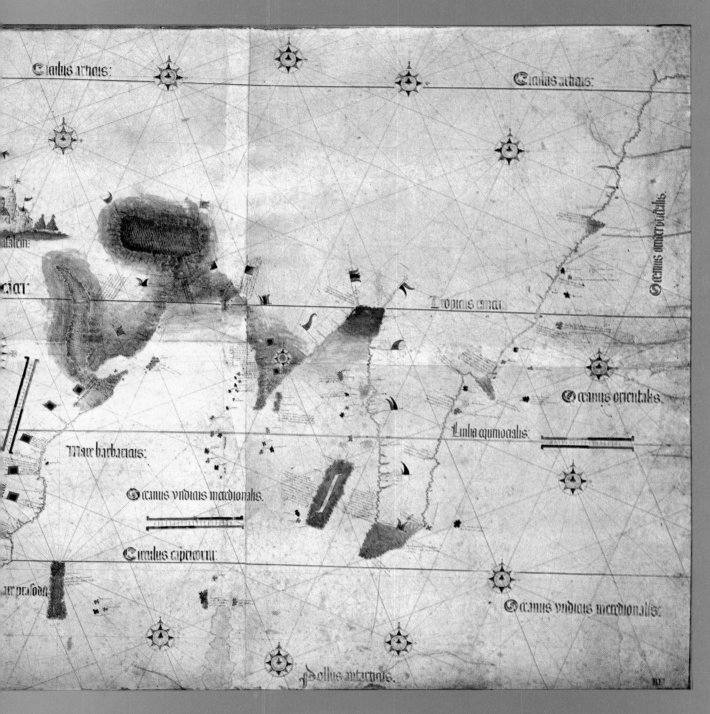

separate continents, not an extension of the Asian mainland.

Delicately illuminated flags and legends mark the voyages of Cão, Dias, da Gama and Cabral. The inscriptions entice the daring. The East was full of places like Toporbana, near Sumatra, "the greatest island found in the whole world and richest in everything."

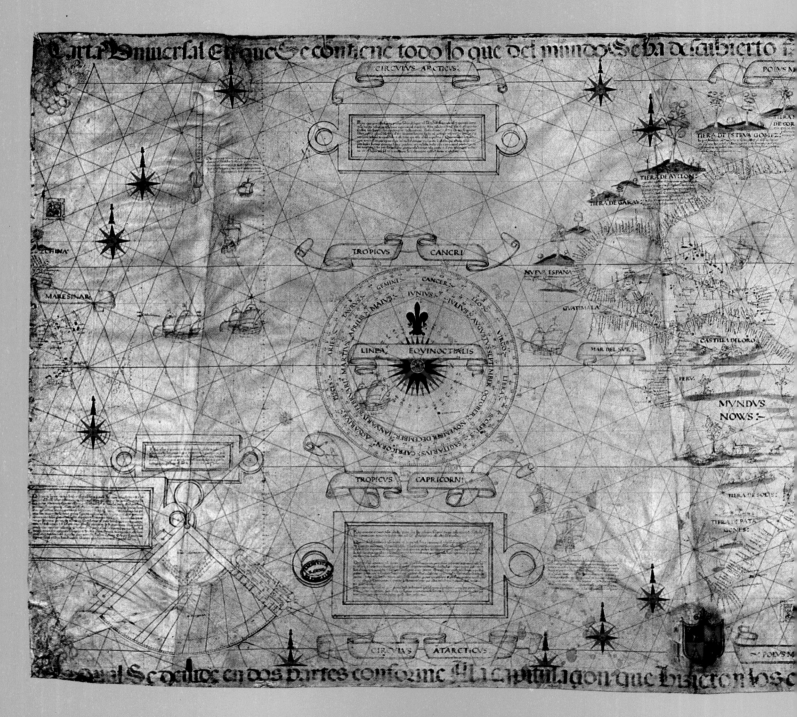

A mapmaker's memorial to discoverers of the sea

"All the world that has been discovered up to this time." The grand description placed on this chart by Diogo Ribeiro is an honest statement of fact.

Ribeiro's copy of the latest Portuguese *padron*, made in 1529, marks a high point in the history of ocean exploration. Dias, Columbus, Vespucci and da Gama had completed their voyages, and the survivors of Magellan's fleet had come home to Seville only seven years earlier. All their splendid accomplishments are recorded here.

The world is larger now than anyone suspected. What the cartographers did not know—as can be seen on the diagram at right—they left blank. Their Africa may be too broad, India too narrow and the eastward reach of Asia too expansive, but the mapmakers can hardly be blamed. The explorers' navigational knowledge and instruments,

like the astrolabe and quadrant that decorate Ribeiro's work, were not yet equal to the exacting task of locating longitude. However, what the cartographer did accomplish is remarkably precise. His chart, as the words of a later historian attest, stands as "the finest of all memorials to the discoverers of the sea."

First giant stride on the route to India

 thousand miles southwest of Gibraltar the bleak Sahara pokes a lifeless finger into the Atlantic at Cape Bojador. Nothing grows there—not even weeds. There is no sign of life. From the northeast, a constant wind blows, whipping up sand devils and fearsome waterspouts, pushing up giant rollers from the Atlantic to gnaw at the desolate red sandstone cliffs until they collapse into the ocean in clouds of spray. For 20 miles offshore, the oily sea is shallow—scarcely six feet deep—milky with suspended sand and swept by powerful currents. Lying there under an incandescent sun, the cape could easily be a nightmare vision of the end of the world. And for a thousand years, that is what Cape Bojador actually was to a Europe sunk in the terror-filled sleep of the Dark Ages.

Medieval Europe believed that at Cape Bojador men came so close to the sun that their skins were roasted black and the sea boiled away into slime crawling with grotesque monsters. It was a place where the coastal hills were made of a mysterious lodestone that would draw the metal fastenings out of a ship's planks, sending sailors to their doom. Even those adventurous spirits who thought there might be something beyond Cape Bojador were reluctant to skirt the point by shaping a course far out to sea—for then they risked sailing off the edge of the world.

This terrible fear of the cape and what might or might not lie beyond lasted all through the 14th and into the 15th Century. No truly enlightened men on the eve of the Renaissance thought that the world was flat or that the sea boiled, but enlightened men were few in number. For the majority—peasants, serfs, fishermen, sailors and even many guild merchants, scholarly clerics and chivalrous knights—the world was filled with vulgar superstition, clotted with ignorance and brimming with demons to discourage anyone from venturing beyond his own feudal village, much less into the vast and trackless seas.

Then, early in the 15th Century, Cape Bojador was boldly challenged. From a retreat high on the headland at Sagres in southern Portugal, a wealthy prince of the royal household, a younger brother of the ruling king, dispatched the first of many ships to probe south along the African coast in search of a passage to India and the Orient, where untold treasure was dimly perceived to lie. Austere, ascetic, totally immersed in his "school" of mapmakers, geographers, astronomers, seafarers and wanderers from the farthest reaches of the Mediterranean, this prince—who would be known as Henry the Navigator—sought not only a way to the riches of the Orient but also some means of establishing an alliance with the mysterious Prester John, who was believed to rule a fabulous Chris-

The twin towers of the royal palace of King Manuel I crown the skyline of 16th Century Lisbon, rivaled only by the Carmo Church on a neighboring hill (upper left). On the banks of the broad Tagus River the tower of another of the King's palaces rises above the royal orange grove (bottom left), while in the river itself a flotilla of both lateen- and square-rigged vessels as well as oar-powered galleys plies back and forth. Although the painting is contemporary, it is embellished with scenes (far left and right) of a siege of the city that took place in the 12th Century.

tian kingdom somewhere in Africa or Asia. Together they would deal a death blow to Moslem infidels, who controlled trade routes with the East and barred Christians from the Holy Land.

At first, Henry's thrusts into the southern sea were destined for disappointment. "Although he sent out not only ordinary men but such as were of foremost name in the profession of arms," wrote Henry's personal chronicler, Gomes Eannes de Zurara in 1453, "yet there was not one who dared to pass Cape Bojador." In 1433 Henry sent out one of his own squires, a brave, sturdy and experienced man named Gil Eannes. But Eannes sailed only as far as the Canary Islands, far short of Cape Bojador, took some captives and returned to Portugal. Henry prepared another ship, and the following year sent Eannes forth once more, urging him to "strain every nerve to pass that cape. You cannot find a peril so great that the hope of reward will not be greater." Added Zurara: "The Prince was a man of very great authority, so that his admonitions, mild though they were, had much effect on the serious-minded."

Now Eannes sailed south and, swallowing his fear, gave Bojador a wide berth by heading southwestward far out to sea. After many days he found favorable winds and shaped a return course east. At last the explorer sighted land and, anchoring in a small bay, went ashore. The place was uninhabited and dry, but less barren than Cape Bojador. There were plants flowering in the dunes behind the beach. Gil Eannes uprooted a bouquet and took it back to Prince Henry, saying, "Since, my lord, I thought that I ought to bring some token of the land since I was on it, I gathered these herbs which I here present to your grace, the which we in this country call roses of Saint Mary."

Eannes had landed on the bleak littoral, 100 miles south of Cape Bojador, on what is today known as the Western Sahara. Thus in one simple but terrifying step Portugal had overcome a monumental obstacle to discovery, one that for centuries had confined Europeans to the familiar security of their coastal waters. For nearly 60 years thereafter, inspired by Prince Henry, Portugal alone would press forward in search of a sea route. She would then be joined by Spain in an intense rivalry that would change the world for all time.

Sailing out from the Tagus River at Lisbon, a handful of Portuguese explorers would pass Cape Bojador and inch their way south to define the west coast of the unknown African continent. Then on their heels four of history's greatest explorers would take the measure of virtually the entire world. These towering discoverers—Bartolomeu Dias, Vasco da Gama, Christopher Columbus and Ferdinand Magellan—would come and go in a mere instant of time, barely 35 years from first to last. But in those few breathtaking years, they would discover that Europe was not a medieval land mass surrounded by paradise and purgatory as shown on the maps of the day, but rather one small continent in a world of continents. They would find that all the seven seas were interconnected, and that all men's dominions were accessible by sea.

By the beginning of 1487—53 years after Gil Eannes rounded Cape Bojador—Portuguese explorers had probed Africa's west coast all the way to Namibia but no Portuguese ship had yet found the continent's

Sea serpents, such as the ship-consuming monster depicted in this 1558 Swiss engraving, were deemed a real hazard by early mariners, whose mortal terror fired their fantasies. In his chronicles, Swedish Archbishop Olaus Magnus recorded sightings of a giant sea snake that "puts up his head on high like a pillar, and catcheth away men, and he devours them."

elusive southern tip; the Atlantic Ocean had yet to be crossed; the existence of the Americas and of the great island-studded Pacific Ocean was still undreamed of. But by the end of 1522, ships were regularly sailing east around Africa to India and the Orient, and west across the Atlantic to the Northern and Southern hemispheres of the New World.

Dias, da Gama, Columbus and Magellan were not the only makers of this revolution, but they were the pathfinders who made it possible. Dias, the least remembered of the four, rounded southern Africa to open the sea route from Europe to the Indian Ocean. Da Gama took the first trading fleet from Europe to India, establishing a base for the expansion of empire to the Spice Islands of the Pacific. Columbus, in discovering the Caribbean and Central America, opened the way for conquest and empire throughout the Western Hemisphere—and Magellan, first to enter the Pacific, proved that men could sail around the entire world.

None of the explorers ever grasped the full meaning of their achievements. Often they mistook them entirely. Their motives, in the main, were no loftier than wealth and power. Only ruthless ambition and the will to triumph—coupled with seamanship of the highest order—carried them through. They survived every hazard known to the sea: hurricanes and typhoons, ice, shipwrecks, mutiny, marooning, native attacks, thirst, hunger, scurvy and a devil's handful of other diseases.

The ships they sailed were a recent marriage of northern Europe's square-riggers and the lateen-rigged vessels of the Mediterranean—a combination that made it possible to sail much more effectively into the wind. It was an innovation that enabled the explorers to probe into seas that had previously been inaccessible, or to make their way home after venturing far downwind along unfamiliar coasts. But the ships they sailed were nevertheless tiny, foul and overcrowded. Often they were old and leaky as well. Their primitive maps and navigational instruments could lead to errors of hundreds of miles. By any logic they faced impossible odds. Small wonder that they still loom larger than life, for in the end their achievement was not only the opening of the entire world in one generation, but the wiping away of a millenium of ignorance.

The Portuguese seafarers who first rounded Cape Bojador in 1434 perceived Africa to be far more than merely a vast obstacle in the route to India and the Orient. The great Dark Continent stretching endlessly south had been an object of fascination—and no little fear—to European peoples for centuries. Few strangers ventured far into the awful searing wastes of the Sahara. But from time immemorial small bands of daring men had put to sea and (before Cape Bojador attained its awful reputation) sailed down the West African and East African coasts, seeking to unfold their secrets. They had returned laden with treasure and brimming with tales of strange phenomena and even stranger beings.

As early as 2000 B.C. ships of the Egyptian pharaohs had nosed south along the coast of Somalia and Kenya to bring back slaves, great tusks of ivory, exotic animal skins, gold and rare woods. The Greek historian Herodotus records that in the Fifth Century B.C. the Egyptian Pharaoh Necho sent a crew of Phoenicians on an extraordinary voyage of exploration around Africa clockwise: "Setting out from the Red Sea, the Phoenicians sailed into the Indian Ocean. Each autumn they put in at whatever point of Africa they happened to be sailing by, sowed the soil, stayed there until harvest time, reaped the grain, and sailed on; so that two years went by and it was not until the third that they doubled the Pillars of Hercules and made it back to Egypt. And they reported things which others can believe if they want to but I cannot, to wit, that in sailing around Africa they had the sun on the right side."

Though it strained the great scholar's credulity, the account has the ring of truth; the statement about the sun being on the opposite side below the equator could only have been made by somebody who had experienced it—for nobody had ventured that far south before.

It is also said that around 500 B.C. Hanno of Carthage took 60 galleys filled with colonists through the Strait of Gibraltar and down the west coast of Africa to found a second empire. How and when Africa swallowed these settlers is hidden by the mists of time. But Hanno survived, and related that on the outbound voyage they "coasted along a country with a fragrant smoke of blazing timber, from which streams of fire plunged into the sea. In the center a leaping flame towered above the others and appeared to reach the stars. It was called the Chariot of the Gods." The likelihood is that Hanno's Chariot of the Gods was the 13,353-foot Mount Cameroon, tallest in West Africa—which Portuguese captains would look upon with awe 2,000 years later.

In exploring the Red Sea, the Romans discovered a water-borne route to an undreamed-of world far to the east. During the rule of Caesar Augustus, 120 Roman ships each year sailed from Africa's Red Sea coasts south and then east to India's Malabar Coast, riding the southwest monsoon eastward from May to September, and returning on the northeast monsoon from November to March. And there are indications that the Romans journeyed farther still, by sea up the coast of Vietnam to southern Chinese ports.

The profitable explorations of the ancients brought wide knowledge of navigation and geography, and encouraged much speculation as to the true nature of the world. By 500 B.C., the Greek mathematician Pythagoras had concluded that the earth was a sphere, and by 200 B.C. another Greek mathematician, Eratosthenes, calculated the circumference of this sphere accurately to within 200 miles. In the Second Century A.D., the Hellenized Egyptian astronomer, mathematician and geographer Claudius Ptolemy charted Europe, Asia and Africa roughly according to their latitude and longitude; he reported, accurately, that if the globe were cut into four equal parts "by the equator and one circle through the poles, the extent of the part inhabited by us is very nearly enclosed in one or the other of the northern quadrants."

In the Fifth Century the Dark Ages fell upon Europe. Visigoths from the north sacked Rome, and Vandal armies smashed across Europe to North Africa. The light of classical scholarship flickered and went out. Some knowledge survived in the hands of the Catholic Church, and some found a home among the Moors of Islam, who were pressing westward from Mecca across the Middle East and North Africa into Iberia. Yet these two repositories of knowledge were virtually closed to Europeans in the Middle Ages. The Church regarded many classical manu-

Marco Polo's window on Cathay

"It must be known then that from the creation of Adam to the present day, no man, whether pagan, or Saracen, or Christian, or other, of whatever progeny or generation he may have been, ever saw or inquired into so many and such great things as Marco Polo." So in 1299 declared the Italian writer Rustichello of Pisa in the prologue to his account of the travels of Marco Polo. Entitled *The Description of the World*, the book recounted a series of remarkable journeys spanning 20,000 miles and 24 years—and reopened medieval Europe's slumbering eyes to the fabled lands of Asia and the Orient.

Born into a prominent family of Venetian merchants, Marco was scarcely 15 years of age in 1271 when he set out with his father and his uncle, Niccolò and Maffeo Polo, on an awesome journey to the lands of the great emperor Kublai Khan, in China.

From Venice the Polo trio sailed to what is now Turkey, where they struck out overland into the Asian wastes. On the first leg, Marco marveled at many things: Mt. Ararat, where Noah's ark was said to have grounded, the three Magi's tombs in Persia, and particularly a curious black oil that seeped up from the ground near the Caspian Sea and was "not good to eat," he later reported, "but is good for burning."

The Polos trekked across the Pamir Mountains at an altitude where "no birds are to be seen," Marco observed, and "fires when lighted do not give the same heat." Continuing eastward, the three travelers entered the Gobi desert,

Marco Polo, as pictured in 1477

At Hormuz, merchants prepare to cross the Arabian Sea to India. The illustrations here and on the following pages are from a 1375 copy of Polo's book.

A headless man with his face on his chest, and an armed cyclops stroll past a one-legged creature who rests on his back, using his single gigantic foot as a sunshade. Popular European lore placed such monstrosities in the wilds of Asia, and though Marco Polo never mentioned such bizarre creatures, they inhabited other popular travel books of the time, and somehow found their way into an illustrated edition of Polo's book.

The magnificent palace of Kublai Khan in China, surrounded by white stone walls 25 feet high, towers over verdant palace grounds where richly clad nobles ride on magnificent chargers. "The building is altogether so vast, so rich and so beautiful, that no man on earth could design anything superior to it," Polo declared.

With the Khan presiding, officials issue paper money in exchange for a merchant's silver bullion, a transaction that amazed Polo because paper currency was virtually unknown in Europe at the time.

where night winds moaning across the searing sands became siren voices, luring unwary travelers off the trail to perish. "Even by daylight men hear these spirit voices," Polo said, "and often you fancy you are listening to the strains of many instruments, especially drums, and the clash of arms."

It was not until 1275, four years and some 7,000 miles after departing Venice, that the travel-worn trio reached the walled palace of Kublai Khan, in Cambaluc, the site of present-day Peking. The great Khan received them warmly. At banquets, he presided over 40,000 guests and innumerable servants, Polo said, displaying staggering wealth and splendor.

Soon after their arrival, the Polos witnessed the Khan's observation of the Tartar New Year, which began on the first day of the Christian calendar's February. On this day the Khan and his subjects dressed in white, deemed the luckiest of colors, for a pageant featuring an awesome parade of 5,000 elephants, each laden with huge casks of the Khan's treasure. "I can also assure you for a fact," Polo recalled, "that on this day the Great Khan receives gifts of more than 100,000 white horses, of great beauty and price."

Kublai Khan had no compunctions about employing capable foreigners in his service, and the Polos soon won his confidence. He appointed the young Marco a kind of inspector general to tour and report on the state of the vast khanate. Traveling south through China as far as Burma, and later venturing east to the sea, Polo came upon crocodiles, he said, that had mouths "big enough to swallow a man at one gulp." No less alarming were some of the human inhabitants: one tribe completely covered with tattoos, another "addicted to eating human flesh, esteeming it more delicate than any other."

On China's east coast Polo came across a curious seafaring custom. Before setting sail, the ship's crew would often send "some fool or someone who is drunk" aloft in a huge kite to determine the ship's fortune. If the kite rose straight up, the ship would be lucky. If it did not rise or crashed, the ship was deemed unlucky—like the man in the kite—and was kept in port that year.

So able and observant was Polo that the Khan sent him to India to inquire of religion there—comparative theology was one of the Khan's passions—and to purchase a begging bowl thought to have belonged to the Buddha himself. A secondary mission was to buy a ruby said to be the world's largest.

Polo sailed to India in a fleet of great four-masted junks, one of the few true oceangoing vessels at the time. Along the way he visited Sumatra, where he made a discovery of enormous commercial importance—"all the precious spices that can be found in the world."

Polo found the great ruby coveted by the Khan on the island of Ceylon, off the tip of India. The stone, he reported in awe, measured "about a palm in length and the thickness of a man's arm, glowing red like fire." But alas, the Ceylonese ruler refused to part with his treasure, and Polo returned to the Khan's capital empty-handed.

By now, 17 years had passed since the three Polos had arrived in China. They were becoming homesick, and petitioned the Khan to return home. With some reluctance the aged Khan allowed his trusted Venetian advisers to depart. The journey home took three years, the travelers arriving in Venice in 1295—and finding, according to legend, that their startled relatives did not recognize them. But recollection came swiftly when the seams of their Tartar garments were ripped open and a fortune in jewels tumbled forth.

While the Polos were celebrated in their native Venice, it is only by a quirk of history that a formal record was ever inscribed for all the world to know. In 1298, Marco Polo was captured in battle against Genoa and spent a year in prison. It was there that he met Rustichello. Over the months, Polo related—and Rustichello committed to paper—the astounding tale of the years at the court of the Khan.

The resulting volume, hand copied at first but later printed, fired the imagination—and lust—of nations, and did much to call forth the great age of the explorers. And in the end, such men as da Gama and Magellan could attest to the truth of Polo's statement shortly before he died in 1324: "I did not write half of what I saw."

At the port of Cambay, India, crewmen unload ships while merchants dicker over the price of Cambay's cotton, leather goods and indigo. Wherever he went, Polo noted local wares and trade conditions. "You must know that in this kingdom there are no corsairs; the people live by trade and industry and are honest folk."

scripts as pagan heresies, and the Moors were utterly disinterested in sharing maps and logs with the hated Christians.

Only the Venetians, on their island city-state in the Adriatic, maintained trade relations with the Islamic powers. Canny and pragmatic, Venetian merchants developed a lucrative trade with the Moslems, who in exchange for glass, woolens, coral and coin readily sold the goods of both Africa and Asia. The might of Venice hindered the rest of Europe from participating directly in this fabulous trade. But the more Europe heard of it, the more tantalizing it all appeared.

In the early 13th Century, the Venetian traders Maffeo and Niccolò Polo and Niccolò's son Marco traveled overland to the court of the Khan in China, and returned to fire Europe's lust and imagination with tales of their travels *(pages 23-26)*. In Marco Polo's account of the treasures of the Sea of China he said: "It contains 7,448 islands, most of them inhabited. And I assure you that in all these islands there is no tree that does not give off a powerful and agreeable fragrance and serve some useful purpose—quite as much as aloewood. There are, in addition, many precious spices of various sorts. The islands also produce pepper as white as snow and in great abundance, besides black pepper. Marvellous indeed is the value of the gold and other rarities to be found in these islands."

In different circumstances it would have been simple enough to redevelop trade with Africa and retrace the Polos' overland route to the Orient. But overland access was denied, both by the Moslems and by the jealously monopolistic Venetians. To awakening Europe, the broad seas were the only answer. But in all of Europe, only one nation and only one man were to prove equal to the challenge. That nation was Portugal. That man was Prince Henry the Navigator.

A small and barren land with a lengthy coastline, Portugal inevitably found its fortune in the seas. "If Spain is the head of Europe, Portugal, where land ends and sea begins, is the crown upon the head," sang the country's greatest national poet, Luis de Camões in 1572. The roots of Portugal's greatness at sea were fishing and trade. Salt fish was a staple of medieval diet, both in the Mediterranean and along the Atlantic, and tuna, so abundant off the Portuguese coast, was an ideal fish for salting. Yet the Portuguese were never content merely to trade. Like the Spaniards, they regarded themselves as duty bound to carry on the crusade against the infidels of Islam, with their Military Order of Christ—the successor to the Order of the Knights Templar in Portugal—leading the fight. Portugal's crusading zeal in time would find two principal outlets. One was by military assaults on the Moors in North Africa. The other was in outflanking the whole of Islam and opening a great new trade route, first to Africa and then around that huge continent to the Indies.

Surprisingly, the man who focused Portugal's great energies and ambitions never embarked on a single voyage of exploration himself. Prince Henry the Navigator could in no wise be termed a practicing mariner. The third son of King João I, Henry was taught literature, statecraft—and war. At the age of 21 he distinguished himself in an attack on the Moors in North Africa, and remained for several years as governor of captured territory there. It was from North Africa that he dispatched his first tentative explorations, including one in 1419 that resulted in the discovery of the Madeira Islands. Seven years later, at 26, Henry became grand master of the militant Order of Christ, and henceforth he was able to apply the Order's great treasure to what had grown into his life's passion; moreover, it could be argued that the Order was doubly served because the voyages down the African coast were a means in part of crusading against the Islamic Empire.

With one foot in medieval Europe and the other in the Renaissance— half crusading knight, half classical scholar—this pivotal figure at the dawn of the age of exploration seems never to have been comfortable with the conflicts raging inside of him. Although he spent his days with worldly men at his school at Sagres, Henry lived in strict celibacy. Intensely religious, from the time he took up the cause of discovery until he died an old man, he wore a rough hair shirt beneath his princely trappings—an act of penance that may have served as a constant reminder of his singular mission in life: his campaign against the Moslems.

From the very start, Henry had a powerful idea of the shape of his world, of what might be found in Africa and of how resolute men might conquer the continent's surrounding seas. If any layman in Portugal was privy to the ancient knowledge locked in the vaults of the church it was he, a prince of the royal household, a holy crusader against infidels. Henry also had present knowledge; he had heard that Moorish traders had ventured across the Sahara to bring back both gold and slaves from richer, more fertile lands to the south. He was determined that Portugal should have both, and gain them by the sea.

It is not recorded how much treasure Henry expended or how many seaborne expeditions he sent south to Africa during his 40 years as Portugal's towering sponsor of exploration. But there were dozens before Gil Eannes finally turned the continent's fearsome Cape Bojador in 1434—and there were scores afterward as Portuguese exploration burgeoned. For Henry, Africa was the goal and the prize. As the years passed, his explorers at first ventured cautiously past Cape Bojador, then surged southward in ever-increasing jumps. In the process they rediscovered the geography known to the ancients, and clasped for themselves the treasure previously monopolized by the Moors. They erected monuments to the glory of God as they went, and they littered the beaches with their shattered ships and battered bodies. And in the end, they turned the continent and sailed northeastward toward India.

The great southern adventure got under way slowly. In 1435, only one year after Gil Eannes had rounded Cape Bojador, Henry called once again on that bold and daring seafarer, sending him and another intrepid captain named Afonso Gonçalves Baldaia farther south than any Portuguese ship had gone before. The two explorers sailed 50 leagues beyond the cape—and there came upon the footprints of men and camels in the dunes above the beach. Then they returned to Portugal and reported the exciting find to Prince Henry. He took it as proof of the tales he had heard about the Moors finding life and treasure in the west of Africa. "It is evident," said the Prince, "that the inhabited region cannot be far off. Or perchance they are people who cross with their merchandise to some

In an Indian market a bullock bearing water bags is surrounded by an inventory of Eastern flora. Men gather jasmine blossoms, while a woman displays betel leaves, more blossoms, tropical fruits and one sprig of pepper. Below, sketches from a 1597 English plant guide show four spices—by no means used only for seasoning. Pepper, advises the guide, "is good against poison," cinnamon eases the "frettings of the guts," cloves "comforteth the heart," and nutmeg "is good against freckles in the face."

PEPPER   CINNAMON   CLOVE   NUTMEG

seaport with a secure anchorage for ships to load in.'' Henry immediately sent the captains forth again with orders to "go as far as you can, and try to bring news of these people. Capture one of them, if possible. To me it would be no small thing to have some man to tell me of this land."

The captains immediately sailed south and, anchoring in a likely bay, sent two young men reconnoitering inland on horses brought for the purpose. Before long, the horsemen came upon a group of spear-carrying Africans among the rocks and dunes. But instead of making peaceful overtures, the horsemen galloped toward the Africans, sending them fleeing in terror, never to be seen again. Bitterly disappointed, the Portuguese cruised on farther south along the coast to an inlet they named the Rio do Ouro, the River of Gold, assuming that it was the river where Prince Henry had told them the Moors traded goods for the precious metal. But what awaited them instead were vast herds of large, sea-dwelling mammals that they called sea wolves—a name later explorers changed to sea lions.

"On the bank at the mouth of the river was a great multitude of sea wolves, about 5,000," recorded Zurara. "Afonso Gonçalves caused his men to kill as many as they could, and with their skins he loaded his ship—for, either because they were very easy to kill, or because the bent of our men was toward such an action, they made among those wolves a very great slaughter."

The skins were of a dense, finely textured fur, and were well received by Henry and his brother King Duarte. Soon a brisk trade in African skins and animal oils was bringing profit to Portugal.

But it was not until 1441, five years later, that the Portuguese were able to capture the human treasure that Henry was seeking in Africa. That year the Prince's chamberlain, Antão Gonçalves, sailed to the Rio do Ouro and, after filling his hold with skins, decided to venture inland with a squad of stalwarts. They had gone only a short distance before they saw, as Zurara reported, "a naked man following a camel, with two spears in his hand." As the Portuguese approached, the lone tribesman brandished "those arms of his right worthily and began to defend himself as best he could. But Affonso Goterres wounded him with a javelin, and this put the Moor in such fear that he threw down his arms like a beaten thing." Later that day, the Portuguese found a woman walking in the dunes and captured her as well. Before they could set sail with their captives, an armed caravel arrived, bearing the young Portuguese knight Nuno Tristão; he decided that Prince Henry would be even more pleased with many more captives. "Besides the knowledge that the Prince will gain by their means," Tristão said, "profit will accrue to him by their service or ransom."

In short order, the adventurers found two encampments of natives and charged down upon them on horseback yelling the traditional battle cries "Santiago!" (invoking the Apostle Saint James) and "Portugal!" Ten prisoners were seized, among them a chief named Adahu, who the Portuguese guessed must be a member of African nobility because of his fine clothes and proud bearing. Tristão was so delighted with the taking of so many captives that he knighted the chamberlain on the spot, making Antão Gonçalves the first Portuguese to win such honors in Africa.

Though the sum total of his seafaring amounted to a few crossings of the 14-mile-wide Strait of Gibraltar, Prince Henry of Portugal won renown as "The Navigator" for his lifelong support of Portuguese exploration. By combining the quest for empire with a crusader's sense of Christian mission, Prince Henry sought to fulfill his personal motto, "The Desire to Do Good" inscribed, in French, below this contemporary portrait.

31

The return of the two ships to Lisbon with captives effectively silenced growing criticism of Henry's enterprises as a waste of money. The prisoners were invaluable as a source of information about Africa, how the coast lay and what opportunities for trade might exist. But that was the least of it. The country had been seriously short of manpower ever since the Black Death, and the prospect of armies of slaves created so much enthusiasm that Henry had no difficulty finding captains and crews for his voyages. The great European slave hunt had commenced.

On his next voyage, Nuno Tristão reached the island of Arguim, where he was greeted by a fleet of 25 canoes filled with tribesmen. The chronicler Zurara reported that they "journeyed in such a wise that they had their bodies in the canoes and their legs in the water, and used these to help them in their rowing as if they had been oars. And our men had had so little experience, when they saw them from a distance, they thought it might well be that they were birds, in a part of the world where other marvels greater than this were said to exist." Closer scrutiny revealed the truth of the matter to Tristão, and his men managed to capture 14 of the canoe people. Portuguese feelings were mixed, reported Zurara: "First of all the pleasure they had was very great to see themselves thus masters of their booty, of which they could make profit, and with so small risk; but on the other side they had no little grief, in that their boat was so small that they were not able to take such a cargo as they desired."

Under the eager encouragement of Prince Henry, discovery thereafter proceeded hand in hand with slavery. The mouth of the Senegal River was reached in 1445 by one Dinis Dias, a noble squire of João I, and the following year Tristão found the Gambia River. Numerous captives were taken on each voyage, and by 1448 trade in slaves had become so heavy that Henry ordered a fort and trading post built on Arguim Island off Cape Blanco, the first European trading post to be established overseas. By this time, King Duarte had died, and Henry's older brother Pedro had been appointed regent until the child-king Afonso V reached his maturity. With fraternal generosity, Pedro gave Henry a charter allowing him to keep the one-fifth share of all profits from African voyages that normally went to the Crown. Despite the wealth of the Order of Christ, Henry for some years had been feeling the pinch of the cost of his enterprises. Now they were at last beginning to pay for themselves in gold and slaves, and the royal fifth brought Henry substantial profits.

The slaves were not received with unalloyed satisfaction—at least in some quarters. The chronicler Zurara observed that large numbers of the captives on the slave ships were women and children "not able to run so fast"—and Zurara himself was moved to tears by the spectacle of the slave market at Lagos: "What heart could be so hard as not to be pierced with piteous feelings to see that company? For some kept their heads low and their faces bathed in tears, looking one upon another; others stood groaning very dolorously, looking up to the height of heaven, fixing their eyes upon it, crying out loudly, as if asking help of the Father of Nature; others struck their faces with the palms of their hands, throwing themselves at full length upon the ground; others made their lamentations in the manner of a dirge, after the custom of their country. To increase their sufferings still more, there now arrived those who had charge of the divisions of the captives, and who began to separate one from another, in order to make an equal partition of the fifths; and then was it needful to part fathers from sons, husbands from wives, brothers from brothers. No respect was shown either to friends or relations, but each fell where his lot took him."

There were times when the trade posed perils for the slavers. At the mouth of the Senegal River in 1445, reported Zurara, a diminutive Portuguese squire named Stevam Affonso crept stealthily up upon a Guinean who was hard at work—"and the intentness with which the Guinea labored, he never perceived the approach of his enemy until the latter leaped upon him. And I say leaped, since Stevam Affonso was of small frame and slender, while the Guinea was of quite different build; and so he seized the Guinea lustily by the hair, so that when the Guinea raised himself erect, Stevam Affonso remained hanging in the air with his feet off the ground. The Guinea was a brave and powerful man, but though he struggled very hard, he was never able to free himself, and so strongly had his enemy entwined himself in his hair that the efforts of these two men could be compared to nothing else than a rash and fearless hound who has fixed on the ear of some mighty bull. While those two were in their struggle, Affonso's companions came upon them and seized the Guinea by his arms and neck in order to bind him. And Stevam Affonso, thinking that he was now taken into custody, let go of his hair, whereupon the Guinea, seeing that his head was free, shook off the others from his arms, flinging them away on either side, and fled."

As the Portuguese pushed ever farther south, a new and promising coastline began to unfold before the bows of their caravels and *barchas*. As the bleak Saharan shores receded, they emerged into the lands of equatorial Africa: fearfully hot, but lush, well-watered and rich looking. "They saw a country very different from that former one," reported Zurara, "for that was sandy and untilled, and quite treeless, like a country where there is no water—while this other land they saw to be covered with palms and other beautiful trees."

In 1445, Diego Afonso erected a large cross of wood known as a *padrão* to mark the passage of Cape Blanco, a headland of white cliffs 425 miles south of Cape Bojador. It was the first of the great *padrões* in Africa, signifying the claim of Portugal to these new lands and serving as mileposts for those who followed the first explorers. Within 43 years, they would dot the whole coast of Africa for 7,000 miles southward.

Now, as the Portuguese ventured farther and farther from home on voyages lasting many months, conditions aboard their tiny ships became oppressive. Of the 20 to 30 men aboard a 50-foot-long *barcha* or a slightly larger caravel, only the ranking officers and noblemen might have the luxury of a tiny cubicle of a cabin aft. The ordinary seamen lived on the open deck, sheltered from the sun in the shadows of the sails, curling in corners to escape the rain squalls and tearing winds. At that, it was preferable to going below into the stinking hold. Even the briefest chore belowdecks was odious: food rotted within days in the heat of the tropics; rats, lice, maggots and other vermin thrived in the bilge, the rats steeping everything in urine and peppering the boat with droppings. Captains ordered the crew to splash salt water onto the boards to kill the stink, as fishermen had for centuries. Stomachs had to be strong in any case because many of the ships were rolling in their sea-gait, and all were built to ride the waves and not slice through them.

On leaving Lagos, the ships carried fresh fruit—lemons, oranges—but these were consumed within a few weeks. Garlic cloves in large amounts were carrïed both for their imagined medicinal qualities and for awakening palates stupefied by the tedium of salted meat and fish hardened to the texture of pine bark, and biscuit and unleavened bread crawling with weevils. Wine, usually of the worst quality to begin with, went bad as voyages drew on, but gave some relief, and was carried in generous quantities. It also helped to deaden the pain when gums and joints began to swell with scurvy. Idle hours were passed in drinking and card games; when one crew saw a black mountain inland, they named it Ponta Negra—Black Point—because a sailor engaged in a card game called *manille* had just played a black trump.

On their voyages, the Portuguese increasingly took along African captives, whom they had sought to Christianize and train as agents. The thought was to put these loyal tribesmen ashore in their homeland, so they could win over their peoples and build trade for Portugal—in both goods and slaves from other tribes. The scheme suffered an initial setback in 1443 when the chief Adahu, captured two years before by Tristão and Gonçalves, was returned to the Rio do Ouro and simply vanished. The Portuguese were dismayed because they had lavished great care on Adahu as a nobleman and had treated him with all proper chivalric regard. But other captives, handsomely treated at Prince Henry's stronghold near Sagres, returned to their home villages and were instrumental in bringing about the cooperation of a number of African tribes. Some of these men had been successfully Christianized; others retained their religion but were nevertheless content to work for Portugal. In both cases, they helped in increasing the amount of gold shipped out of Africa and in opening new markets for Portuguese goods. They also brought many slaves captured from tribes in the interior.

On one occasion, a Portuguese captain returned to Henry's court with ostrich eggs. Though the eggs were at the very least several weeks old by the time they reached Sagres, they were served to Henry, insisted Zurara, "as fresh and as good as though they had been the eggs of any domestic fowl. And we may well presume that there was no other Christian prince in this part of Christendom who had dishes like these upon his table."

The new African trading market was so promising by the 1450s that Henry was leasing exploration and trading rights to entrepreneurs and taking out a percentage of the profits. Afonso V had now reached his maturity and ruled in fact as well as name. But the new king was interested only in waging war against the Moors and left Henry a free hand to extend his explorations. And among those who petitioned the Prince for a license to explore and trade was a 22-year-old Venetian merchant-adventurer named Alvise da Cadamosto, who charmed his way into Henry's confidence. Cadamosto was typical of the Europeans now beginning to arrive in Africa. These men were not explorers in the sense that Eannes, Tristão and the other early captains were; they were entrepreneurs seeking trade more than discovery. Cadamosto in 1454 opened

The fruitless hunt for Prester John

Prester John, fabled Christian king, holds an elaborate cross in this illumination taken from a 1558 map of Africa.

When the first Portuguese explorers set forth for Africa and the Orient, one of their goals was to find the legendary kingdom of Prester John. According to centuries-old lore, this was a Christian land of great wealth and power situated somewhere in the South or East. An alliance with its ruler would not only assure vast trade, but would place the hated Moslems between two mighty jaws of Christianity—or so medieval Europeans believed for four long centuries.

The origins of the legend of Prester John are obscure. But the tale gained great currency in the year 1165 when a letter addressed to Emperor Manuel Comnenus, Christian ruler of the Byzantine Empire, appeared mysteriously promising deliverance to Europe from the Moslems pressing in on all sides. "I, Prester John, who reign supreme," the letter said, "exceed in riches, virtue and power all creatures who dwell under heaven. Seventy-two kings pay tribute to me. I am a devout Christian, and everywhere protect the Christians of our empire." The letter continued: "Honey flows in our land, and milk everywhere abounds." There was even a river, the letter said, containing "emeralds, sapphires, carbuncles, topazes, chrysolites, onyxes, beryls, sardonyxes and many other precious stones."

Comnenus apparently did not act upon this letter, but as copies circulated throughout the Christian world, the kingdom of Prester John became an object of great and continuing fascination. At first it was thought to lie in India, then in central Asia, but the travels of people like Marco Polo in the early 1300s demonstrated the error of that idea. Attention next focused on Africa when the missionary Jordanus of Sévérac returned from the East with word that the kingdom of Prester John was in Ethiopia.

In 1493 a Portuguese agent named Pero da Covilhã, traveling overland, managed to reach the court of the Ethiopian king. But he was forced to remain there, and it is unclear whether or not an account of his findings filtered back to Europe. In any case, in 1527 another Portuguese, Francisco Alvares, returned home after a journey to Ethiopia. He reported that the King was a believer in Christ and moderately wealthy: "He had on his head a high crown of gold and silver." But alas, he was a mere youth of 23 who called himself Lebna Dengel, not Prester John, and he ruled a primitive nomadic people in a rugged domain that was scarcely a land of milk and honey.

Europe's disappointment was less than shattering. For by then Columbus had discovered a New World, da Gama had reached India by sea and Magellan's crew had circumnavigated a globe that held real marvels far more breathtaking than those in the legend of Prester John. And what of the letter that had fired Europe's imagination for so long? Its origin remains obscure, but whether it was a hoax by a mischievous scribe or an innocent fantasy, its author could never have imagined its spectacular impact.

his account of his African travels with a refreshingly frank appraisal of his objectives: "My constant attention was in the first place to acquire wealth, and secondly to procure fame." He may or may not have acquired wealth. But he did achieve a measure of posthumous fame, for his journal, published in Venice in 1507, was avidly read for its description of the budding trade empire the Portuguese were nuturing in Africa.

Sailing south to Arguim, Cadamosto described the trading base: "You should know that the Prince has leased this island of Arguim to Christians, so that none can enter the bay to trade with the Arabs save those who hold the license. They have dwellings on the island and factories where they buy and sell with the Arabs who come to the coast to trade for merchandise of various kinds, such as woolen cloths, cotton, silver, and cloaks, carpets and similar articles and above all, corn, for they are always short of food. They give in exchange slaves whom the Arabs bring from the land of the Blacks, and gold dust. The Prince therefore caused a castle to be built on the island to protect this trade for ever."

With such protection, Cadamosto noted, the Portuguese could sail to the island year round, without fear of being waylaid by any Moorish pirates who might be lurking along the coast.

In the next four years, Portuguese navigators explored the coast southward as far as Sierra Leone. They were now more than 1,300 miles from Cape Bojador, and it seemed that the elusive ultimate cape of Africa might be just ahead: at that point the coast angled sharply eastward.

But in 1460, before anyone could find out, their patron and sponsor of 40 years of unprecedented exploration, Henry the Navigator, died of an unidentified illness at age 66. He was buried in the hair shirt he had worn all his life. Thanks to this great man's genius, power and persistence, Europe had broken out of its medieval shell and embarked on a quest for the ends of the earth. In Henry's lifetime, Portugal had begun to look outward toward empire, and by the time of his death it was impossible to turn back. Portugal now controlled African coastal trade, and had proved that exploring for profit was eminently practical. Although the elusive cape remained undiscovered, it was now within reach.

The years passed after Henry's death—and still no one had rounded the cape. Coasting ever eastward along the Gulf of Guinea past the mouth of the Niger and on to the Bight of Biafra through the 1460s, Portuguese captains discovered nothing to contradict Ptolemy, who had indicated a huge gulf—Sinus Hesperus, or Bay of the Evening Star—bitten out of the West African coast. The coast then swung southward again. In 1471 the Portuguese crossed the equator and advanced as far as the prominent Cape Santa Catarina. But without Prince Henry the voyages did not proceed with the singlemindedness necessary to achieve the final stroke. For 20 years, King Afonso V concentrated his energies on waging war with the King of Fez in Morocco.

But while Afonso V had never taken an active interest in voyages of discovery, his son João, an active and imaginative child, was raised in a court filled with tales of great adventure on the high seas and along the African coast, of vast riches in gold and slaves, of the untold wealth of the Orient lying just around Africa's tip, of the legendary Christian king

Prester John, and of the immense advantages that would accrue to Portugal if the monopoly of Venice and Islam on trade with Asia could be broken by a new sea route.

While still in his teens, the youth was put in charge of African trade by his father. And when Afonso V died in 1481 and his son, at age 26, was crowned João II, he quickly set about with remarkable single-mindedness achieving the imperial goals that Henry, his great-uncle, had so long sought. To achieve this, João first had to secure his kingdom: he ruthlessly asserted royal control over Portugal's nobility—forcing the feuding and ambitious families of the kingdom to swear drastic oaths of obedience on threat of death. He proved himself to be a man for his age, beheading the duke of one troublesome household and slaying with his own hand the chief of another. Thereafter, João II commanded unswerving loyalty throughout his realm.

João's first African mission was to dispatch engineers to build a powerful fortress on the coast of Guinea, São Jorge da Mina. But Mina was not intended merely to defend what Portugal had already seized for herself: it was also to serve as a base for new discoveries. João hoped to encounter Prester John and enlist him in the attempt to take the Indies trade away from Venice and Islam, as the chronicler Lopes de Castanheda makes clear: "Along that coast, it seemed to him, he would be able to discover the dominions of Prester John of the Indies of whom he had heard; so that by that way it would be possible to enter India and send his captains to fetch those riches which the Venetians brought for sale."

To make certain that nobody mistook Portugal's claim, João had his captains take along limestone route markers—great seven-foot columns, carved with his coat of arms, the dates of the voyage and the King's name and that of the explorer, surmounted by a limestone, metal or wooden cross. These *padrões* were mounted on prominent headlands where they could be seen easily from passing ships.

Perhaps reflecting João's own determination, the captains who sailed for him were of a new breed, not content to venture only a few score leagues into the unknown on each voyage.

One of these, Diogo Cão, proved himself the greatest explorer Portugal had yet known. No individual commander had ever pushed so far. In the course of two voyages spanning four years, each entailing high courage and incredible hardship, Cão added another 1,450 miles of Africa to the map, reaching the Congo and sailing up this stupendous river for several leagues, then returning and cruising south down an increasingly inhospitable coast as he neared the Namibian desert. The journeys were profitless in terms of gold, slaves or other commercial possibilities; rare among his colleagues, Cão seems not to have cared for such matters, but to have entered into his travels with the sole purpose of discovery over the greatest distance possible. Little or nothing is known about him personally, reflecting perhaps the secrecy that João, ever alert for spies of Venice, applied to the great missions under way. Among the few surviving accounts of Cão's discoveries is one from Duarte Pacheco Pereira, a Portuguese captain who participated in the founding of Mina in 1481, and in the subsequent voyages down the coast. They are terse in the extreme: "The Negroes of this land are poor people who cannot maintain

Tantalized by the possibility of reaching India by circumnavigating Africa, King João II of Portugal sent out the explorer Diogo Cão and later Bartolomeu Dias with orders to follow Africa's uncharted coastline as far as they dared before turning back. João's personal symbol (upper left) was the pelican, chosen in honor of his wife; it was considered a noble bird and a symbol of motherhood.

themselves or live except by fishing, of which there is much here; they are idolaters. In this land there is no profit."

It was recorded on another occasion that on one of his voyages Cão sent some of his crew inland to contact the king of the Congo; the crew vanished and were found alive three years later when Cão himself returned and made friends with the king. But details of the adventure are singularly absent.

It is known, however, that in January 1486 Cão placed his last *padrão* at the southernmost point he reached in Africa: Cape Cross, 50 miles north of Walvis Bay in Namibia, only a short voyage from the southern tip of Africa. Cão had come close to final success, and had ventured farther than any other Portuguese explorer into latitudes where his shadow fell to the south. On his way back to Lisbon he died, of causes and circumstances unknown.

Several years passed and then, in 1487, Cão's mission was resumed by a man who would at last fulfill the hopes of Henry the Navigator. His name: Bartolomeu Dias.

Dias also remains an enigma—perhaps for the same reasons of royal secrecy. There are no portraits of him, no date of his birth, no details of

The Gold Coast fortress of São Jorge da Mina was erected in 1482 by João II as a trading post and a supply base for his African explorers. Although the walls there were quarried from local outcrops, everything more complicated—fitted stone for its doorways and window recesses, hewn timbers and tiles—was laboriously brought 4,000 miles from Portugal.

his family or early career, although it is possible that he was related to Dinis Dias, the first to round Cape Verde in the service of Henry, more than 40 years earlier. It is also possible that he is the same Bartolomeu Dias exempted from paying dues on ivory brought back from Guinea in 1478, and that he participated in the establishment of Mina in 1481, commanding one of the ships sent to build the fort. But Bartolomeu Dias was a common Portuguese name, akin to William Smith or Edward Jones in England, and these accomplishments may have been the work of several different men.

In any case, when Bartolomeu Dias the explorer set sail from Lisbon in August 1487, it is clear that João had commissioned him to make a major voyage, because among the vessels in the small fleet was a wide-beamed supply ship to carry additional food and fresh water for a long journey. The supply ship was old and expendable, so that it could be burned for its iron fittings if necessary before the fleet turned back. The chronicler João de Barros described the flotilla:

"Two ships are armed and another to carry excellent stores, since many others had returned from discovery for want of supplies; the captaincy was given to Bartolomeu Dias, gentleman of the house of Dom João who was one of the discoverers of this coast." With Dias on his caravel was the pilot Pero de Alemquer. The other caravel was captained by João Infante, a young knight, with the pilot Alvaro Martins. The wallowing supply ship was captained by Dias' brother Pero. Altogether some 50 or 60 men made up the complement of the three ships. Among the passengers were six Africans—two men, four women—who had been brought to Portugal from southern Africa by the redoubtable Cão. The Africans were to be landed as emissaries of Portugal, the women handsomely dressed and bearing samples of gold, silver and spices. Aside from gaining the confidence of African tribes with an eye to trade, they were to try everything possible to locate Prester John. Women were often chosen for this duty on the assumption that they would not be drawn into tribal wars.

Dias was furnished with a new map specially prepared at King João's order, incorporating the latest intelligence about the geography of Africa and the Indian Ocean. Several months earlier, in May 1487, João had dispatched a Portuguese spy named Pero da Covilhã overland to Asia to find trade routes and to look for Prester John. The map given to Dias was identical to Covilhã's. Because of the timing of the two missions, it may be that João hoped that the two men would meet in India.

Dias sailed his two caravels and supply ship south to Mina, restocked and proceeded south to Angra das Aldeias on the coast of Angola, where Cão had first captured the African men aboard. There the two were set ashore among their friends. The supply ship apparently was left in this comfortable anchorage, where there were abundant supplies of fish, and fresh water. Nine men remained aboard as guards.

Passing Cão's southernmost *padrão* at Cape Cross on the 1st of December, the two caravels coasted south along a barren countryside of dunes—the beaches crowded with gulls and cormorants, the shallow sounds and estuaries choked with reeds—and on into the unknown.

On December 8 they anchored in Walvis Bay, protected from the roll-

Erected by Diogo Cão at Cape Cross in 1486, this seven-foot limestone column surmounted by a cross was one of a dozen similar monuments planted along the African coast by Portuguese explorers. Known as padrões, they bore the royal coat of arms as well as an inscription announcing that the king had "ordered this land to be discovered."

ers sweeping in from the South Atlantic by a peninsula five miles long, a place of fabulous bird life: flamingos, wild geese, pelicans and clouds of sea birds wheeling over the green waters. Nearby were Hottentot villages of conical huts made of bullock hides, whose inhabitants herded cattle and sheep and could down sea birds with their longbows.

In another fortnight they covered the 250 miles to the harbor now known as Lüderitz, which Dias called Angra das Voltas—the Bay of Tacks. Dias had been clawing his way against a stiff southerly breeze for days, and his two caravels were able to anchor in Lüderitz only after tacking laboriously against these head winds. The southerly kept them in Lüderitz another five days, during which Dias put ashore one of the four African women aboard.

When the winds finally shifted, the caravels poked south along a coast studded with rocks, some of which extended far offshore, forcing Dias to shy out to sea for safety, and they passed the mouth of the Orange River without noticing it. Some 10 miles offshore, in late December, 1487, the caravels again encountered head winds. Distant mountains hove into view: the Lombada da Pena, later called Kamiesberg, and on January 6, 1488 the Serra dos Reis—Range of the Kings—which was probably the steep, red-hued Matsikamma heights north of the Cedarberg in modern Cape Province. Although they did not realize it, the mariners were within 200 miles of the cape they had so long and so arduously sought.

This was Dias' last sight of land on the west coast of Africa. For after passing the Serra dos Reis in a constant struggle against the mounting southerlies, the Portuguese broke for open ocean and ran far out to the west. Dias apparently lost patience with his painful crawl against the head winds, which had lasted for the better part of a month, and decided on the basis of long Atlantic experience that favorable following winds might be found out of sight of land. The chronicler Barros suggests that a violent northerly drove the caravels off, but such freakish northerlies are almost unknown in January, the South African midsummer.

For 13 days the ships plunged south-southwest, quartering into an ever-strengthening gale, their sails lowered to avoid dismasting. They were pounding through cold, mountainous seas in the Roaring Forties before Dias gave the command to swing east and search for the coast again. In his head he was carrying the navigator's triangle: his last estimated landfall on the coast, the distance covered during the run out to sea, and the time it should take to fall in with land again. But the time calculated to reach land came and went. No land loomed on the eastern horizon. Dias shifted course again, this time to the northward, before the wind. At last, at the beginning of February 1488, his weary and increasingly fearful crews sighted Africa again. But now the coast was running east, not south. They had rounded Africa's southern tip without realizing it—and for the moment without quite being able to believe it.

Dias cruised eastward, and the coastline continued to stretch farther and farther east. There could be no mistake. Even by their crude navigational instruments they could calculate that they were 2,000 miles east of Cape Bojador, almost due south of Egypt for that matter, with open sea to the south. Ptolemy's picture of Africa as a land mass joined to Asia at the Malay Peninsula had been totally demolished. And from the look of it,

this was a fair land, bracing yet temperate, showing glimpses of plants and trees that reminded the crews vividly of Portugal.

They saw the mouth of a river where cattle were grazing under the care of herdsmen. Dias named it the Rio dos Vaqueiros—the River of the Cowherds—but did not land because of the heavy surf. On February 3 they sailed past great cliffs containing a huge cave, and Dias christened it São Bras, for the festival of Saint Blaise, who lived in a cave. Beyond the cape was a bay that Pacheco Pareira later described: "Within this bay is an islet close to the land on which are many very large seals which have shoulders and necks and manes like lions. Also on the islet are many sea birds, larger than ducks, covered with feathers, but without any plumes in the wing, so that they cannot fly, and those who hear the voice of these birds think that it is an ass braying"—they were jackass penguins. He proceeds to describe a river flowing into the bay and its "many reeds, rushes, mint, wild olive trees and other plants and trees not like those of Portugal."

According to the pilot of the lead caravel, Pero de Alemquer, Dias and his crew landed and were able to barter trinkets for sheep and cattle, giving the crew its first fresh meat for months, but when Dias tried to take on fresh water from a well dug close to the beach he was pelted with

Venturing round the southern tip of Africa, Bartolomeu Dias and his men were the first Europeans to gaze on the geological curiosities of the Cape of Good Hope, including Table Mountain (background, center) and Lions Head (left). The landmarks would serve future explorers, like the Dutch in this 17th Century engraving, as the turning point in their voyages to the East and back.

stones. In response one of the crew felled a tribesman with a crossbow shot, and the Africans fled inland with their cattle. Pacheco Pereira later warned of dealing with the natives there. "Whoever goes to this place must beware of the Negroes of this land because they are very bad people, and several times they have tried to kill the crews of ships that go there, and he who goes ashore should always be on his guard."

Cruising eastward, the explorers sighted another great mountain range they called the Serra da Estrela because it reminded them of the highest range in Portugal. They caught many fish, and sighted red cliffs, grasslands and lakes, capes and bays. At that point the coast began to turn slightly south of east, and the excitement and enthusiasm of the crews went sour. Had they perhaps not rounded the ultimate cape after all? They anchored in a bay and Dias went ashore on a small islet with a landing party. The men pushed their way through a herd of noisy sea lions and dragged a wooden cross to the 200-foot crest. At its base they celebrated Mass, and christened the islet Ilheu da Cruz.

Once again the coast turned eastward. Barros noted that all was not well aboard: "Here, since all the people were weary and very frightened from the great seas they had passed, all with one voice began to complain and demand that they should go no farther, saying that as their provisions were being exhausted they should turn and search for the ship they had left behind with their stores, which remained so far away that when they reached her they would all be dead from hunger. That it was enough for one voyage to have discovered so much coast, and it would be better counsel to turn to discover the great cape which appeared to be behind them, to say nothing of going on."

In order to satisfy the complaints, Dias held a council of the officers and some of the principal sailors. He asked what would be the greatest service to their king. All agreed that they should return to Portugal, and Dias asked them to draw up a document to this effect.

Dias explained that he himself wished to press forward, and that he had only conferred with the officers and crew because the King had instructed him to do so on matters of importance. When they had all signed the document, Dias asked them if they would be willing to go up the coast for two or three more days. If they found nothing, they could then turn, he promised, and sail for home.

The ships raised anchor, passed Algoa Bay and Bird Islands, and followed the coast as it swung farther and farther to the northeast. On the third and last day, the caravels were riding off the mouth of a river, the Keiskama. To the great disappointment of Dias, rough seas and a roaring surf made it impossible to land there with a *padrão*, which should have marked this historic spot. But as soon as he could after turning back, Dias landed to erect the *padrão* on the summit of Kwaaihoek, a dark-faced promontory standing boldly out against the white sand of the coastline. Dias left the cross there, a slim and lonely column on the desolate hill above the Indian Ocean, according to Barros, "with as much pain and sentiment as if he were leaving a beloved son in eternal exile."

Though they were now homeward bound there was still vital work to be done: charting the section of coast they had missed during the outward detour into the South Atlantic. Six weeks after leaving Kwaaihoek the caravels anchored in Struys Bay, east of Cape Agulhas, in the last week of April 1488. Here in stormy weather the greatest swells any of them had ever experienced—indeed the greatest swells in all the world—built up from the Agulhas Bank. The tide was strong and the fog thick, and reefs studded the coast. Dias stayed for three weeks, overhauling the two small ships and foraging for supplies before the long voyage back to the storeship. By the end of May they were at sea again, nosing along the dramatic coastline approaching the southermost point of Africa. On June 6 they reached a "great and noble cape" with granite crags standing out far to sea, flanked by Table Mountain and rock spires. This was the tip of the continent, one of the earth's most dramatic landfalls. There Dias placed the second stone *padrão* of his voyage, this one to mark the ultimate cape.

Fighting tremendous following seas, the caravels now scudded north around the cape, with Dias keeping plenty of room between himself and the rocks. He declined to follow every contour of the coast north. Instead, remembering that the west coast ran slightly west of north, he kept a northerly course and had no trouble soon sighting the familiar Serra dos Reis of the outward voyage. By Saint Christopher's Day—July 24—his caravels were back in Lüderitz Bay, where he erected his last stone *padrão* before sailing on to the storeship.

Grim news awaited the explorers after their exhausting journey. The storeship was safe. But six of her garrison of nine were dead, murdered by tribesmen attempting to loot the ship. Barros recorded that of the three survivors "one called Fernão Colaço, native of Lumiar, limits of Lisbon, who was a scribe, was so astonished with pleasure upon seeing his companions that he died shortly, being very thin from illness."

Dias was too prudent to risk the homeward voyage with all three ships manned by understrength crews; the caravels took on all remaining provisions and trade goods in the storeship, and she was burned.

One further drama lay in store. As Dias shaped his course across the Bight of Biafra, he called at the island of Principe, where he found another band of Portuguese survivors. They were the remnants of an expedition that had set off to explore the mouths of the Niger, but that had ended in shipwreck. On the advice of the leader of these survivors, Pacheco Pereira, Dias halted on the mainland to barter trade goods for gold, which was then handed over to Crown authorities at São Jorge da Mina. After a welcome break at Mina the caravels set off on the last leg of the voyage home. They returned to the Tagus in December 1488, after a journey of 15 months and 16,000 miles.

They had been to the Indian Ocean and back. At last, the door to the Indies was swung open. The implications for the future were tremendous. The age of discovery had begun and the dream of Henry was being fulfilled. Portugal could now move boldly into the Indian Ocean, bypass the merchants of Venice and the Empire of Islam and lay claim to the treasures of the Orient. Among the tales that would be told, the chroniclers would relate how Bartolomeu Dias went before King João II to tell him of the great African cape—the cape Dias proposed to call the Cape of Storms. Contemplating what lay ahead, João disagreed. Instead, said the young king, it would be called the Cape of Good Hope.

An African craftsman from Benin, modern-day Nigeria, left his impression of a fearsome Portuguese captain, his men and ship—complete with a club-toting lookout in the crow's-nest—on this splendid, 11¾-inch ivory saltcellar. It dates from the early 16th Century and was probably traded to a Portuguese merchant for guns or for brass, used in artwork.

Evolution of the shipwright's art

The 50-foot Mediterranean lateener (right) carried its long two-spar yard and triangular sail on a mast raked forward and braced to windward by block-and-tackle shrouds. It steered by two oars hung off the stern. The square-rigged northern European knarr (opposite) mounted only one steering oar. When armed, the 55-foot knarr carried castles fore and aft and a small fighting top above the yard.

When the pious northern warriors of the Third Crusade sailed through the Strait of Gibraltar on their way to the Holy Land in 1189, they found the Mediterranean teeming with vessels quite different from their own. The most obvious differences were to be found in the manner of rigging and in the method of hull construction.

The Mediterranean ships were distinguished by a large triangular sail slung fore and aft from the mast and supported by a slanting yard sometimes longer than the ship itself *(below)*. The crusaders called these ships lateeners after the Latin countries where they were used. The fore-and-aft sail that the crusaders saw probably originated in the Indian Ocean and reached the Mediterranean during the Arab conquests in the Seventh Century.

With its long elegant yard slicing into the breeze, the lateener could sail much closer to the wind than could a ship rigged with square sails such as those on the crusaders' knarr *(below, right)*. As a result, the lateener was not kept

waiting in port at the mercy of the weather; it could tack its way out to open sea in the face of almost any wind. Coming about, however, presented some difficulty. The heel of the yard had to be hauled in to the base of the mast and then passed across to the opposite side of the ship, and the shrouds, which supported the mast only on the weather side, also had to be switched every time the sail was sheeted home on a new tack.

Just as there were certain disadvantages to both the lateen rig and the square rig, there were pluses and minuses in the different methods of construction—lapstrake in the ships from the north, carvel-built in the Mediterranean (right). No doubt both the crusaders and the Mediterranean seamen thought their own ships superior, but the ships that 300 years later would carry Columbus across the Atlantic and take Magellan on his circumnavigation of the globe would be a product of the crossbreeding of these two distinct traditions of shipbuilding.

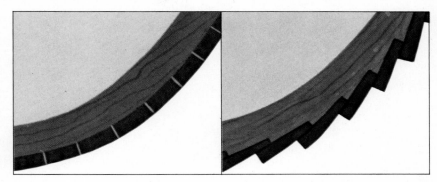

The carvel hulls of Mediterranean ships were built by laying planks edge to edge on a preconstructed framework (left), securing them with wood pins and caulking the gaps. In the north, ships were lapstraked: the planks were overlapped and riveted to each other. A notched rib was then fitted against them on the inside face of the hull.

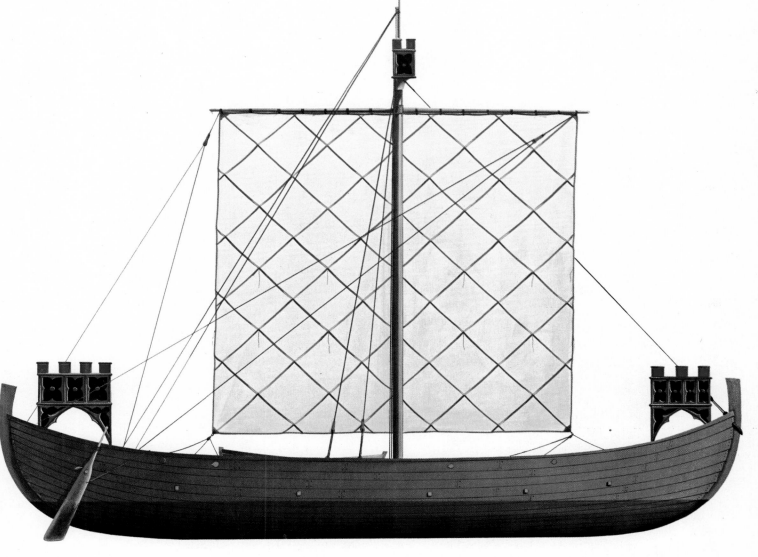

A decided advance over earlier models, this 13th Century two-masted lateener built for the Crusades was big enough at 86 feet to carry 100 men plus a crew of 30 or 40 and their equipment on its two decks—indicated here by rows of deck-beam butts protruding through the side planking. Its masts were stepped in wooden chimneys to provide more support, especially for the 40-foot, precariously mounted foremast.

Size from the south, innovation from the north

When the Ninth Crusade was getting underway in 1286, its leader, King Louis IX of France, ordered his transports built at Genoa and Venice, and from records of this transaction it seems that Mediterranean shipbuilders had begun cashing in on the main advantage of their carvel-style construction: size. The preconstructed frames of the carvel-built ships could support huge hulls, and the lateeners built for Louis had two full decks, with half decks running from midships to the bow, and two or three quarter-decks in the stern for cabins. Such vessels required great power, and now, two masts were secured to the keel, both with huge lateen sails.

At about that time, a new ship had come into being in northern Europe (right). Though its rigging remained essentially like that of its predecessor, the knarr, the elegantly curved sternpost was replaced by a straight one and, most important, a rudder was hung down its centerline, eliminating unwieldly steering oars and greatly increasing the helmsman's mechanical advantage. For the next two centuries, these ships, called cogs, taxied northern Europeans and their goods from city to city and to the Mediterranean, where the cog's merits did not go unnoticed.

Representative of the durable and versatile work horse of the late Middle Ages in northern Europe, this square-rigged cog measured 130 tons, with a stout hull that was 77 feet long and a wide 24 feet on the beam. Her sides were still lapstraked for simplicity, but the strakes, instead of being set into a keel, were joined to a flat bottom made of planks laid edge to edge and caulked. This cog with its single square sail was easily managed by a crew of 10.

48

The ultimate lateener, this 70-foot
15th Century caravel mounted three raked
masts. The hull was carvel built, with a
light displacement, and there was
no superstructure in the prow to interfere
with the sweep of the main yard's
heel. Outriggers fore and aft provided a
fastening point so that the sails could be set
more efficiently into the wind.

A caravel to beat against the wind

The premier vessel of discovery in the 15th and early 16th centuries was a light, swift lateener called the caravel *(below, left)*. Bartolomeu Dias, Vasco da Gama and Christopher Columbus all depended on it. Derived from small offshore fishing craft of the western Mediterranean, the caravel combined the important merits of the stern rudder and the straight sternpost common in northern Europe with the nimbleness of the Mediterranean lateen rig. Its shallow draft made it ideal for exploring coastal waters.

Easily handled by only a 25-man crew, the caravel could also be rerigged *(below, right)* to incorporate the virtues of square sails whenever needed: excellent speed before a following wind and ease of handling in foul weather. This version was called a *caravela redonda*. Such was the caravel's versatility that the Portuguese often boasted that while other ships could make the long voyage to Guinea, no other craft but a caravel could make it home again against the prevailing winds of the African coast.

A combination of designs, this 70-foot caravela redonda, as square-rigged caravels were called, was ideal for making downwind runs. And explorers could transform a three-masted lateen-rigged caravel on the spot. The mainmast was restepped to be perpendicular to the deck. The center mast from the quarter-deck was jumped to the bow and became the square-rigged foremast, while the mizzen stayed lateen. Sails were remade from old ones and bent on cut-down yards.

With a bulky, carvel-built hull of 86 feet and a burthen of 100 tons or more, this 16th Century nao needed all the canvas it could muster to propel it. Unlike lateeners with only one sail to a mast, the square-rigged nao could hang two or more sails on a mast. As a result, new sails such as the main-topsail above the fighting top were introduced. A spritsail, used for maneuvering, was hung under the bowsprit and a good-sized lateen was kept on the mizzen for working into the wind.
The yards were run up and down the mast on collars of large beads called parrels.

Full rigged for circling the globe

Although the trim little caravels performed yeoman service throughout the age of discovery, the farther explorers reached out from home the greater became the need for a bigger, beamier craft with more room for men, supplies and trade goods. This new vessel would have to combine the strong points of both northern and Mediterranean designs. It would have to be square rigged like the cog, for on the high seas a vessel would most often be running before a prevailing wind and the square rig did this best. It would also have to be big and this meant stepping two or three masts, as on the Mediterranean lateeners. It also would have to be of carvel construction.

The full-rigged ship was born to answer these demands. The Portuguese called it the nao and in a slightly larger version throughout the Mediterranean it was known as a carrack. Magellan, when he set sail from Seville in 1519, had a fleet composed entirely of naos, which had more room for the men and provisions and spacious holds to accommodate precious cargoes of spices. By the middle of the 16th Century, these three-masted, multisail vessels, with their distinctive overhanging forecastles and round sterns, were accepted as the most seaworthy ships afloat. For all their ungainliness, they were the ship of the future, and every successful oceangoing merchantman or warship built in Europe for the next three centuries would hark back to them as progenitors.

Chapter 2

West from Spain to a vast New World

The Virgin of the Navigators spreads a protective cloak over Christopher Columbus, kneeling together with the ships' officers who accompanied him on his epic voyage to the New World and some of the natives he brought back with him. Below the cloud-borne assemblage in this 1505 painting is a fleet of vessels: at center, a nao like the explorer's flagship, the Santa María, dominates the scene. Around it are three galleys, two lateeners, two ships' boats and another nao.

he year 1492 was a momentous one for Spain. On January 2 a dark and bloody era came to an end as the city of Granada, the last great Moorish stronghold in Europe, capitulated to Christian armies after 750 years of uneasy coexistence, and a decade of terrible struggle. The Catholic sovereigns, Ferdinand and Isabella, having unified Spain, rode in triumph through throngs wildly cheering "Granada! Granada for King Ferdinand and Queen Isabella!"

In 1492, as well, a great scholar, Elio Antonio de Nebrija, the "light of Salamanca," famed far and wide for his studies in theology, law and, above all, rhetoric and linguistics, published his *Art of the Castilian Language,* the first grammar of a modern European language. He presented a copy of his work to Queen Isabella, to whom it was dedicated. When she inquired for what purpose the grammar might be used, one of her courtiers replied, "Your Royal Majesty, language has always been the companion of empire."

That was prophetic. In that same year, on December 25, an explorer for Spain planted the royal flag on an island in a world hitherto unknown to Europe. His feat opened an era in which Spain would surge to the forefront of maritime exploration, and become mistress of an empire of riches such as Western civilization had never known.

Curiously, in an era of burgeoning monarchies and ever more imposing states, this signal venture into exploration came about not by direction from the Spanish Crown, but through the perseverance, in the face of incredible odds and no little humiliation, of a commoner, a foreigner, a strange and lonely figure possessed of a quixotic notion that the Atlantic Ocean was a mere sea, narrow enough to be sailed in a few days' time.

Christopher Columbus was a Genoese weaver's son; he dropped the imperial plum of the New World into the lap of the Spanish Crown because no one else seemed to want it. Sustained only by a sense of divine mission, he had been nursing his grand idea for at least 15 years, and peddling it for eight, before he was able to put it to the test. The Portuguese, to whom he took it first, had shown little interest; after the discoveries of the early explorers sponsored by Prince Henry the Navigator, they were far keener on pressing for India by sailing south and east around Africa. England and France had quarrels to settle between themselves and showed no interest at all. But the Spanish monarchs, after years of fighting the Moors, were suddenly free in 1492 for other undertakings. And they, after a period of agonizing indecision, eventually authorized Columbus' epic voyage west across the Atlantic. The result was to be both a national triumph and, for Columbus, a personal one.

The intimate record of this triumph survives in two very early accounts. Columbus himself kept a detailed ship's log. Though the original journal in the explorer's hand disappeared long ago, its essentials fortunately were abstracted by two men closely associated with him. One was Bartolomé de Las Casas, a chronicler who was a friend of the Columbus family and had access to the explorer's papers. The other associate was Columbus' son Ferdinand. He wrote a sympathetic biography of his father, filled with direct quotations. What emerges from the accounts by Ferdinand and by Las Casas is a touchingly vivid portrait. In

passages where the narrators record moments of success, Columbus'
spirit seems to soar with self-satisfaction. In others, his despair and
frustration seem all too human.

Columbus was an extraordinarily versatile man. He reached the age of
25 illiterate—as did the vast majority of the population of his day—and
then set about learning to speak, read and write in three languages:
Portuguese, the tongue of navigation; Castilian, the parlance of the upper classes in Spain and Portugal; and Latin, the language of scholarship. All the traits that went into this learning process—imagination,
zeal, driving ambition, opportunism and keenness—Columbus brought
to his great mission. These characteristics propelled him out of his life

The crescent-shaped harbor of Genoa—
Columbus' birthplace and boyhood
home—teems with merchant vessels
and warships dressed for action against the
Turks in a 1481 oil by Cristoforo Grassi.
The harassment of southern Italy's
city-states by the Turks drove many
Genoese merchants, fearful for the future,
to emigrate to Portugal, where growing
sea trade offered them new opportunities.

among the lower middle classes into another world, where he could marry a nobleman's daughter, consort with bishops and kings, and seek national backing for his presumptuous project. In Spain, which was in transition out of what might be called the middle ranks among European powers, the destiny of the country and that of the man were to meet.

Columbus had been born in the Republic of Genoa in September or October of 1451, the first of four sons of Domenico Columbo. Outside his father's stuffy shop he could breathe the tangy salt air of the Mediterranean; only a few streets away, he could see the broad harbor of Genoa unfolding to the Ligurian Sea, an arm of the Mediterranean. Running errands in the city, he jostled with boatbuilders, merchants and sailors, and at the quayside he saw mapmakers hawking charts of the Mediterranean coastline. A boy growing up in 15th Century Genoa could hardly escape the lure of the sea—and by his own account young Christopher found it irresistible. "At a very tender age I entered upon the sea sailing," he once wrote his patrons Ferdinand and Isabella. Just how young he was when he went to sea is uncertain, but he may have been only 10.

The first records of Columbus' early years show that around 1471— when he would have been 20—he became a seaman on a Genoese galley chartered by a French duke, and saw brief action in a skirmish with a rival dukedom. For many years he sailed with a noted Genoese shipping family named Di Negri, starting as a deckhand and rising to captain. At least one Di Negri expedition was crucial for Columbus: in May 1476 he shipped westward with a five-ship convoy bound for Lisbon, England and Flanders. Less than three months into the voyage the convoy was mistaken for an enemy force by the Portuguese, and attacked. Columbus was wounded and his ship sank. Hanging onto an oar and paddling as best he could, he crossed six miles of open water. He came ashore on the very coast where Henry the Navigator had established his center of learning—a coincidence that would later seem to Columbus to have been one of many miracles with which his life was blessed.

For someone with the sea in his veins and dreams in his head, Portugal was in any event a good place to come ashore in 1476. That was the decade when Portugal was opening up the Guinea coast to trade. Columbus headed straight for Lisbon, where a large Genoese colony was established. In that community lived Christopher's younger brother Bartholomew, working as a mapmaker. Bartholomew took him in, and before long the two brothers were partners in a mapmaking enterprise.

But mapmaking was not enough to occupy a man of Christopher Columbus' aspirations. He was now 25 years old, and beginning to show a sense of purpose. It was in this period that he set himself to learn to read and write, and to cultivate his social betters. He made a point of going to Mass at a chapel at the Convento dos Santos, a school for aristocratic young ladies, and there he met Dona Felipa Perestrello y Moniz, whom he was to marry. Whatever personal qualities Dona Felipa had to offer, she was more importantly the daughter of Captain Bartolomeu Perestrello, who had successfully colonized Porto Santo, the second largest of the Madeira Islands. By the time Columbus married Dona Felipa, Perestrello was dead, but in his death he had a lasting influence on Columbus. Perestrello's widow gave Columbus the captain's charts, logs and books, a sizable and important library. This was the foundation of a library Columbus himself was to leave his son Ferdinand—who built it into a formidable 15,000-volume collection.

Columbus brought to his reading a decidedly original flair, and left it stamped with his own mark. He made copious marginal notes in a fine and delicate hand. His notes help to document his intellectual growth during those years. Ferdinand believed that it was in the early 1480s that Columbus "began to speculate that if the Portuguese could sail so far south, it should be possible to sail as far westward, and that it was logical to expect to find land in that direction."

Crucial among the books that Columbus read was the *Geography* of Ptolemy, the Second Century Alexandrian astronomer and geographer, who had argued that the known world was part of one Eurasian land mass that stretched halfway around the Northern Hemisphere. It followed that the easternmost reaches of this land mass could be arrived at by sailing westward across the ocean—a conclusion implicit in Ptolemy, and one that was more or less accepted by 15th Century thinkers.

Columbus also read and devoutly believed another book: Marco Polo's *The Description of the World (pages 23-26)*, in which the Venetian traveler glorified the riches of Cathay, where a powerful ruler known as the Great Khan lived in a land of marble-columned bridges; and of Cipangu, which had palaces roofed with gold. Cipangu was one of more than 7,000 islands that Marco Polo claimed were off the coast of Asia—an archipelago so large that it had the effect of extending the land mass of Asia a good 30° farther east than it was by Ptolemy's reckoning. Columbus naturally drew from this the conclusion that Asia was correspondingly closer to the West—by way of the Atlantic Ocean.

There was another spur to the plan forming in Columbus' mind. One of his books was *Imago Mundi* (Image of the World), written in 1410 by Pierre d'Ailly, and published in 1480. D'Ailly, dean of the University of Navarre, asserted that the Atlantic Ocean "is not so great that it can cover three quarters of the globe, as certain people figure it." Columbus eagerly underlined the passage and made a note in the margin to cite d'Ailly's reasoning in arguments over the venerable Ptolemy.

Adding some computations of his own to those he found in d'Ailly's book, Columbus concluded that from Spain to Cipangu the ocean spanned a trim 60°, which he reckoned as 2,400 miles.

By 1484 Columbus was well married, well read and, by one means or another, acquainted with well-known figures. He was also possessed of the idea that India could be reached by sailing west—and he was determined to try it. Making use of associations he had cultivated with Portuguese shipowners—with one of whom he sailed to the new Portuguese fort at El Mina—he obtained an audience with King João II.

Exactly what Columbus proposed to the King has been lost to history—but an insight into the explorer's character was not. The court chronicler João de Barros wrote after the meeting that the King "observed this Christavão Colum to be a big talker, and full of fancy and imagination." Nevertheless, João was sufficiently interested in Columbus' scheme to turn him over to the royal advisers. But with Portugal in the process of fitting out the Diogo Cão expedition—which would get as far as Cape

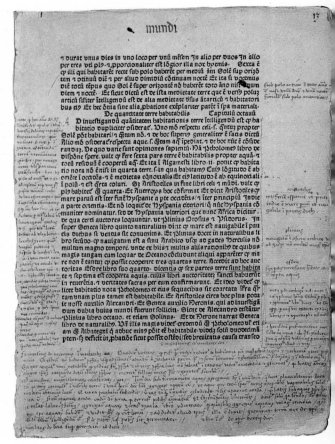

A page from Imago Mundi—a 1410 geography by the French scholar Pierre d'Ailly, who encouraged Columbus by stating that the Atlantic was a relatively narrow sea—has handwritten marginal comments by the future explorer and his brother Bartholomew. Among them is a note in the left-hand margin that records the return of Bartolomeu Dias from the Cape of Good Hope in 1488.

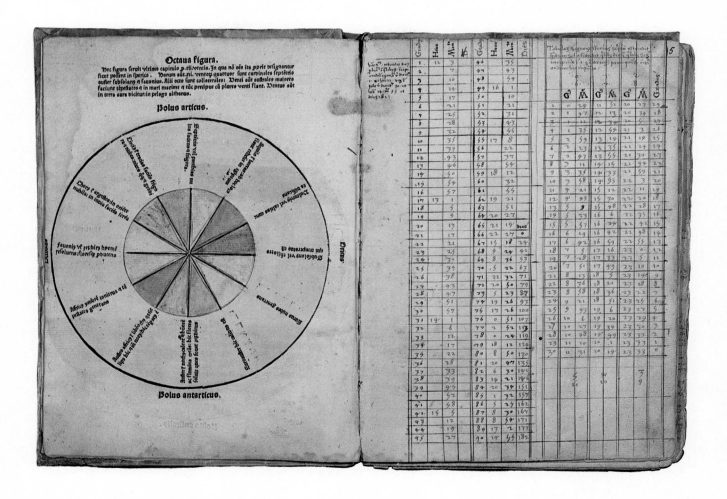

A compass, with coloring probably added by Columbus, and a table of winds and light hours at different latitudes, which he calculated himself, appear on facing pages of Imago Mundi. Columbus may well have carried this volume on his first voyage across the Atlantic; the copious annotations in the book indicate the serious thought he gave in advance to the crossing's navigational problems.

Cross, more than halfway to the tip of Africa—the Crown had little interest in going off on a tangent to the west. In the end, the King's advisers dismissed the Columbus proposal as vain and ridiculous.

At about the time Columbus received this rebuff Dona Felipa died, leaving him with a five-year-old son, Diego. Having nothing to lose, Columbus decided to leave Portugal and try his luck in Spain. He settled in Seville and there did as he had done for a decade in Portugal: he boldly made acquaintances with important people—monks, clergy and nobles. One of them, the Count of Medina Celi, led him to Queen Isabella herself. On May 1, 1486, Columbus went before her and asked the Spanish Crown to back him in a voyage west across the Atlantic.

Queen Isabella, who shared with Columbus the oddity (for a Latin) of having reddish hair, also shared a temperament given to intuitive flashes of comprehension. Although she and Ferdinand were fully occupied with driving out the Moors, Isabella was so strongly taken with her supplicant that she turned him over to a committee of experts presided over by Hernando de Talavera, a bishop who was her confessor and a trusted adviser to the Crown.

Now began an association that, before it was to reap profits for all concerned, was to be the source of great anguish for Columbus, whose zeal for his proposition had become an all-consuming passion.

The young monarchs who underwrote Columbus

Ferdinand and Isabella are justly renowned for setting Spain on the road to empire by sponsoring Columbus. But their accomplishments were far greater than that alone. Before empire there must be a nation, and they were the monarchs who first unified Spain. Their marriage in 1469, when he was 17 and she 18, joined Aragon and Castile, the largest and most powerful Iberian kingdoms—but the Moors still ruled Granada, and the peninsula was pocked with contentious feudal states.

These two were possessed of great vision, and a common determination to implement it. In a decade of violent battle their armies restored Christian rule over Granada, meanwhile developing the first mobile field hospitals in Europe—and massed infantry tactics that made Spain invincible in Europe for 150 years. They ordered new penal codes and organized a police force that became the famous *Guardia Civil*. By shrewdly manipulating royal patronage, they bound the fractious nobility to the Crown and developed a merit-system civil service.

They exerted some control over the mighty Church, engineering the election of a Spanish Borgia as Pope Alexander VI. And in their zeal they also perpetrated the Spanish Inquisition, which, in the name of unity and purity of faith, would torture, imprison and consign to the stake thousands of Jews, Moslems and New Christians.

So alike in mission, the two were opposite in character. Sweetly plump, Isabella was devout and chaste, while Ferdinand was a falconer, jouster and wencher. Her happiness was marred by his infidelity. Yet before Isabella died in 1504, she ordered that they be buried together so that "our bodies may symbolize and enjoy beneath the ground the close relationship that was ours when we were alive."

Adorned in magnificently colored robes, Ferdinand and Isabella radiate piety and ideal purpose in these exquisite 16th Century wood statuettes, which grace the royal chapel in the Granada Cathedral.

According to legend, Isabella used the jewels from this silver- and gold-filigree box to finance Columbus' first voyage. But the tale is apocryphal; even had Isabella been so inclined, a system for funding from a number of sources made the use of the Queen's jewels unnecessary.

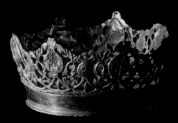

Isabella's silver crown is decorated with open pomegranates, or in Spanish, granadillas, emblems of Granada, whose capture from the Moors in 1492 climaxed the unification of Spain. Her gilded silver scepter bears diving dolphins, symbolizing mighty sea power.

In this bas-relief, an altarpiece in the Granada Cathedral, Ferdinand and Isabella are riding into the conquered Moorish capital at the head of their army. A contemporary observer called the fall of Granada "the most distinguished and blessed day there has ever been in Spain."

The Talavera committee and others that succeeded it deliberated for six years in all. The repeated questions they addressed to the proud and sensitive Columbus made him suffer, in Las Casas' words, "a terrible, continued, painful and prolonged battle; a material one of weapons would not have been so sharp and horrendous as that which he had to endure from informing so many people of no understanding, although they presumed to know all about it."

Columbus comforted himself during this trying time by taking a mistress, one Beatriz Enríquez de Harana. In 1488 she gave him the son Ferdinand whose biography of his father was to be one of the major sources of information about him.

Columbus also cultivated a number of influential friends at court—most significantly, Luís de Santángel, a courtier with irons in many fires. Officially Santángel was Keeper of the Privy Purse for King Ferdinand, who showed less interest in Columbus' scheme than did Isabella. But Santángel was also a calculating businessman with considerable personal wealth, and he was co-treasurer of the Santa Hermandad, a vigilante group that seized the bandits roaming Spain during the Moorish war—and confiscated their plunder.

When after six long years of equivocation the Crown's advisory committee declined Columbus' project in January 1492, it was Santángel who came to the rescue. Granada had just fallen. Spain was overflowing with hidalgos—young nobles who expected land in payment for military services to the Crown. The routing of the Moors left these restless militants without a common foe to unite them—and every reason to fight among themselves, for the Crown had not enough land to go around. The obvious solution, at least to the canny Santángel, was to find new land abroad. But Spain was effectively barred by the Portuguese from finding it in Africa. Spain would have to search in another direction—and that would have to be west, across the Atlantic, as Columbus proposed.

Santángel devised an ingenious scheme, one that could not offend the advisory committee, for scarcely any royal funds would be involved. He suggested to Isabella that he should find the means to finance the voyage west across the ocean with funds he raised from the Santa Hermandad. The project would cost the state only the seamen's wages—and they could presumably come from taxes. Isabella was quick to see the virtues in Santángel's reasoning—and so, now, was Ferdinand.

Suddenly the situation had changed, and everything fell into place. Columbus was fetched for another audience with the Queen and King. This time his plan was approved. What was more, after all those years of waiting, Columbus found his patrons preparing for the Enterprise of the Indies, as they called it, with remarkable speed. Between the Santa Hermandad and some undisclosed sources of his own, Santángel found about 1.5 million maravedis for most of the funding; Columbus himself put up another 250,000 maravedis; and the Crown levied a special tax on the butchers of Seville to provide its share for the seamen's wages. Altogether some two million maravedis went into the undertaking—less than a month's income of one leading Spanish marquis.

By the terms of the contract worked out between him and the Spanish Crown in April 1492, Columbus was to be supplied with three ships, each manned by an experienced crew, provisioned for a year's voyage, and stocked with such trade goods as could be presumed attractive to people in the East—the same sort of beads and bells and bright, shiny but cheap things that Portugal had dispensed along Africa's west coast.

For Columbus the rewards were to be both grand and munificent: the hereditary title of Viceroy and Governor of all the lands he might discover; the rank of Admiral of the Ocean Sea, which would give him jurisdiction over legal and administrative matters of such overseas territories; a tenth share in all the precious stones and metals to be gained by Spain as a result of his discoveries; and an eighth share of the profits of trade. Columbus had demanded all these things, and though they were audacious claims for a commoner to make of the Crown, they were granted.

The fitting out began in May, in Palos, a convenient southwestern port, and home of two prosperous and prominent shipping families, the Pinzóns and the Niños. They provided two caravels—the *Pinta,* a lively, swift-sailing, square-rigged vessel of some 60 tons, and the slightly smaller, lateen-rigged *Santa Clara,* or *Niña* as it was nicknamed. Her tonnage was about 55. A third vessel, the *Santa María,* was chartered from Juan de la Cosa, a Galician who chanced to be in port as the expedition was making up. The actual dimensions of the *Santa María* have not survived, but she was probably a typical nao, with a mainmast taller than the ship was long, and a main yard as long as the keel.

Columbus sailed in the *Santa María.* He drew the fleet's officers and men primarily from Palos and environs, with the Pinzón and Niño families taking several key posts. Martín Alonso Pinzón would be captain of the *Pinta,* and second-in-command to Columbus. An experienced sailor, Pinzón was also a man with a mind of his own, as Columbus would discover. Vicente Yáñez Pinzón, a younger brother of Martín Alonso, was to command the *Niña* with Juan Niño, the owner, aboard as sailing master. Juan de la Cosa remained with the *Santa María* as master, with two of the Niño family in his crew: Peralonso Niño, who signed on as navigator, and the 19-year-old Francisco Niño, who was to act as ship's boy. Altogether there were about 90 men engaged. Among them were a servant for each captain, three surgeons, a secretary, a royal comptroller and an interpreter—an Arabic-speaking converted Jew who was expected to be able to converse with the Oriental potentates they hoped to meet.

On August 3 the little fleet got off to an early start, slipping its moorings as the dawn broke. Before the sun had warmed the decks, the ships had left the estuary of the Saltés and had set their course south before the prevailing northerlies toward the open ocean and Spain's toehold in the Atlantic, the Canary Islands.

On the 10-day shakedown cruise to the Canaries the *Pinta* sprang her rudder and began to leak. Repairing her and converting the *Niña* to a square rig for open-ocean sailing *(pages 70-71)* consumed the better part of six weeks, and when the work was finished, more supplies were taken aboard and the three ships set sail in earnest on September 6.

Columbus' plan was the essence of simplicity. He knew that the Canaries lay in a belt of easterly winds. He believed on the basis of his readings that his next objective, the great island nation of Cipangu, must lie on or near the same latitude, about 28°N. He believed the distance to be about 2,400 miles due west. If he could maintain a 270° course, and an average speed of four knots, as reckoned every half hour by the *ampolleta,* or sand clock, he should be able to find Cipangu in a matter of days: perhaps as little as three weeks.

But Columbus, for all his sublime confidence in his mission, knew that fearsome unknowns lay ahead—unknowns that obviously weighed even more heavily on his crew. He had been underway only three days when he decided to falsify reports of their daily progress—so that if Cipangu lay farther away than supposed, the "people," as he called the crew, would not become afraid and dismayed at the distance they had gone. On September 10, his private reckoning of the day's sail was 60 leagues, some 180 miles, but he said it was only 48; on the 11th he figured 20 leagues but admitted only 16; two days later, he inscribed 33 leagues in his log but spread the word that the ships had sailed only 29.

By one of those ironies of fate, the only man Columbus was fooling was himself. Possibly because he had steadier winds than he had anticipated—and in any event having neither instruments nor wind and current charts with which to compute—he consistently overestimated the *Santa María*'s speed by nearly 10 per cent. Thus the amended figures were generally much closer to the truth than the ones he navigated by.

He was, however, just as eager as anyone to find land and he soon began to think he saw signs of it everywhere. On September 17, when the fleet had been at sea for 11 days, he noted optimistically in his diary that he had seen "a white bird called the boatswain bird, which is not accustomed to sleep on the sea." It is fascinating to contemplate Columbus' identification of this bird, for the species is a strikingly long-tailed neotropical one that ranges far out to sea, wandering north to latitude 40 only in the fall. Columbus almost surely had never seen one before, though he may have heard of them from early Portuguese explorers who could have seen them off Africa. In any case, he was mistaken about their habits; they sleep quite well on the sea and come ashore only to breed.

Another entry on the 19th notes that "a drizzle came without wind, which is a sure sign of land"; again, Columbus was guilty of wishful thinking. Yet he persisted, adding a few days later the encouraging sign that "at dawn two or three small birds came to the ship singing." Next there was a live crab, a whale, a cloud bank such as forms over land, and still more birds, some of them flying westward in flocks.

During all this time, while he and his crew were so earnestly straining to equate the birds, the clouds and the drizzle with land, there was another even more compelling sign. As early as September 16, the diary noted that they "began to see many bunches of very green weed, which had recently (as it seemed) been torn from land, whereby all judged that they were near some island." Actually, they had just entered the Sargasso Sea, a two-million-square-mile plain of primordial algae suspended in the mid-Atlantic. The weeds appeared so thick that the men feared the vessels could not push through—or, as Ferdinand wrote in recounting his father's voyage, "that there might happen to them what is supposed to have happened to St. Amador in the frozen sea that is said to hold ships fast." But they were relieved to find that the clumps parted easily and the ships slid through without impediment.

Family dog at his knee and his mistress, Beatriz Enríquez de Harana, at his shoulder, Columbus sits at table with his two sons. Diego (far left) was his offspring by his deceased wife; Ferdinand (center) was Beatriz' son. They lived together as a family, and the two half brothers were lifelong friends. On his death Columbus charged Diego—who as his legitimate heir would inherit the explorer's property—with seeing that Beatriz "is put in a way to live honorably." Diego not only obliged these wishes, but remembered Beatriz in his own will.

The officers were as tense as the men. Martín Alonso Pinzón was so impatient to see what lay beyond the horizon that he sailed his sprightly *Pinta* on ahead, showing his independence. Another day, Martín Alonso was pacing the poop deck of his caravel, when suddenly he stiffened and shouted out "Land! Land!" Both the *Santa María* and the *Niña* were within earshot and the announcement threw the whole fleet into excited confusion. Some men scrambled up the rigging to see for themselves. Others joined Columbus—who was devout even in triumph—in falling to their knees and reciting the "Gloria in Excelsis Deo." Some of the men jumped into the sea for a refreshing dip—noting happily that dolphins, the sailors' traditional good omen, sported among them. When calm was restored, Columbus ordered the ships to slow their speed and proceed cautiously toward the land; the distance was judged to be about 20 leagues, and it was nearly nightfall. They passed the night in a state of high anticipation. But dawn brought only an empty horizon—and crushing disappointment. The landfall had been a mirage.

Columbus, in his diary, did not mention how the bitter news was received, recording only with simple understatement that "what they had been saying was land was not, but sky." And now, as September verged into October, tempers were beginning to flare and faith in Columbus' judgment sank. On October 6, Martín Alonso Pinzón began to show more of his independence of spirit; he came alongside the *Santa María* and shouted across that they should change course and head southwest by west. Perhaps Pinzón figured that ocean currents had caused them to drift north of their destination. He knew that they had assuredly traveled 2,400 miles. By Columbus' private accounting, they had gone even farther; nonetheless, he rejected the recommendation.

Pinzón fell into line resentfully, only to have Columbus on the next day order a change to west-southwest, noting in his diary that he had seen "a great multitude of birds going southwest." Whether his reason was Pinzón's advice or the flight of the birds, the change was a lucky one. Had Columbus kept to his original course, he would probably have been swept into the powerful north-running Gulf Stream.

By the 10th of October, the fleet was scudding along under a fresh breeze at better than seven knots. But the fact of the fair winds was itself a mixed blessing; one day Columbus noted in his diary that "my people were all worked up from thinking that no winds blew in these waters for returning to Spain"—which would be the ultimate catastrophe. Columbus figured they had sailed 59 leagues, or 180 miles, the previous day, but perhaps growing reckless in his desperation, he reported only 44. He himself took comfort in the weather. "Thanks be to God," he wrote in his journal, "the air is soft as in April in Seville, and it is a pleasure to be in it, so fragrant it is." The crew found no such comfort. "Here the people could stand it no longer," Las Casas says in his *Historia*, "and complained of the long voyage." He added that Columbus "cheered them as best he could, holding out good hope of the advantages they would have." According to Las Casas, Columbus also told them "it was useless to complain"; he intended to continue until he found the Indies.

That took not only fierce determination, but consummate faith in his own mystical vision. His fleet had now been at sea for 34 days. They were

A man of many faces

Italian chronicler Girolamo Benzoni, writing his *History of the New World* in 1565, noted ruefully that if his countryman Columbus had "lived in the time of the Greeks or of the Romans, or of any other liberal nation, they would have erected a statue."

It was true enough that few, if any, monuments were raised to Columbus in his lifetime. So far as is known there was never even a portrait painted of him from life. But at the time Benzoni wrote, more than half a century after the explorer's death, Italian Renaissance painting was coming into full flower, and as the import of Columbus' discoveries became apparent, oils and etchings of the Admiral of the Ocean Sea were fashioned in the hundreds.

By then, of course, because of past neglect, no artist could be certain what Columbus looked like. His son Ferdinand reported that his father "was a well-made man, of a height above the medium, with a long face, and cheekbones somewhat prominent; neither too fat nor too lean. He had an aquiline nose, light-colored eyes, and a ruddy complexion." The chronicler Bartolomé de Las Casas added that he had red hair and freckles.

Those brief words left room for the artists' imagination, so when paintings and etchings of Columbus began to appear, the results were diverse. He was shown in guises that varied from Italianate merchant to Spanish courtier to monastic scholar; from young to old, from lean to plump.

Of the various portraits reproduced here, all from the 16th Century, the one that scholars believe most nearly corresponds to the written accounts is the firm-jawed and sad-eyed ascetic in the large picture below. It was painted in oils by an anonymous Italian artist. The Latin inscription—cropped in the course of four centuries' wear and tear —reads: "Columbus the Ligurian" (Liguria was the Latin name for Genoa), "Discoverer of the New World."

sailing to an uncertain destination with nothing to hang their hopes on but flimsy strands of seaweed and birds that came from nowhere. They were driven by nothing but the will of a contrary commander. In fact, mutiny was close at hand. "They met together in the holds of the ships," Ferdinand reported, "saying that the admiral in his mad fantasy proposed to make himself a lord at the cost of their lives or die in the attempt; that they had already tempted fortune as much as their duty required and had sailed farther from land that any others had done. If the admiral would not turn back, they should heave him overboard and report in Spain that he had fallen in accidentally while observing the stars; and none would question their story." Columbus was saved from mutiny just in the nick of time.

At about 10 p.m. on October 11, Columbus saw what appeared to be a faint flickering light in the distance. It was "like a little wax candle lifting and rising," he noted. This time even he was wary. He mentioned it cautiously to his steward and to the purser; they studied the supposed light, but were not convinced. The ordinary seamen were not told and apparently did not notice the light. But when they were assembled for their nightly devotions, Columbus told them that he would add his own prize of a silk doublet to the royal annuity of 10,000 maravedis for the man who first sighted land.

Four hours passed. Then around 2 a.m. a sailor named Juan Rodríquez Bermejo aboard the *Pinta*—Pinzón's ship was again in the lead—spied the moonlit shore of an island ahead. Ecstatically he shouted out the good news and ran to fetch his captain. Pinzón, giving the signal agreed upon in advance, fired one of the deck cannon to alert the others.

This time they had genuine cause for celebration, Columbus most of all. On a combination of inspired hunch, roundabout logic, garbled facts and, above all, impassioned self-confidence, Columbus had defied the considered judgment of some of Europe's most sophisticated scholars and the bets of a good many hardheaded merchants. And he had won. He had spent an unprecedented 36 days at sea and sailed 2,400 miles across the ocean, and he had found land, exactly as he had promised.

He was certain now that he had reached the Indies. In fact his landfall was Watlings Island in the Bahamas, 9,000 miles from the Indies, with a huge land mass blocking the way between. But 20 years would pass before anyone would know that, and Columbus would never admit it.

Going ashore to claim his prize, Columbus solemnly took possession of the place in the name of the King and Queen. Las Casas reported, "The admiral brought out the royal standard, and the captains went with two banners of the Green Cross, which the admiral flew on all the vessels as a signal, with an F and a Y"—the initials in Spanish of Ferdinand and Isabella. The official embassy went through the ceremony of planting the cross on the beach and naming this first discovery San Salvador—the Savior—"in honor of God, who had pointed it out to him, and saved him from many dangers," his son Ferdinand later explained.

The ceremony was played out before an astonished audience of local inhabitants—amazed but curious and unafraid. Indeed, the ships had no sooner anchored than the island people "all came to the beach, shouting," Columbus recorded in his journal, an action that he devoutly interpreted as "giving thanks to God," just as he did himself. They were in any event eager and cordial; "some brought us water, others things to eat," Columbus went on. Still others "plunged into the sea swimming and came out" to the ships. With animated gestures "they asked us if we had come from the sky."

Columbus' own reaction was one of astonishment. "They all go quite naked as their mothers bore them; and also the women," he recorded. He found the young men, "none of them more than 30 years old, very well built of very handsome bodies and very fine faces; the hair coarse, almost like the hair of a horse's tail, and short, the hair they wear over the eyebrows, except for a hank behind that they wear long and never cut."

The friendly reception accorded by the islanders betokened their way of life. "They bear no arms, nor know thereof, for I showed them swords and they grasped them by the blade and cut themselves through ignorance," Columbus wrote. Noting that some of them had marks of wounds on their bodies, he made signs to ask what they were, and discerned from their replies that there were people on nearby islands who were not so peaceable. Columbus concluded this day's report with the cheerful observation that the docile islanders he had found "ought to be good servants and of good skill, for I see that they repeat very quickly whatever was said to them. I believe that they would easily be made Christians, because it seemed to me that they belonged to no religion."

There was one disappointment, of course. Clearly, this place was not the dazzling Cathay that Marco Polo had described. There were no great cities, no marble-columned bridges, no jewel- and spice-filled bazaars to behold. The land looked stony, scrubby and unproductive, and the people appeared poor for all their good looks and dispositions; they lived in crude huts "with beds and furnishings like nets of cotton," he noted in his diary. (He had seen his first hammocks.) But the poverty did not dismay the optimistic Columbus; he figured that he had landed on one of the 7,448 islands that Marco Polo had counted off the China mainland. He resolved to sail on and explore some more, fully expecting to find Cathay and Cipangu and their wealth. "I was attentive," he wrote on the following day, "and worked hard to know if there was any gold, and saw that some of them wore a little piece hanging from a thing like a needle case, which they have in the nose." Columbus' imagination was fired when the islanders indicated by gestures that to the south there was "a king there who had great vessels of it and possessed a lot."

Columbus decided to do as they suggested and headed south, taking along as guides some friendly islanders with whom he was learning to communicate. Afloat again, he found that there were so many islands marching across the horizon, and all so tantalizing, that he confessed he had difficulty deciding where to go first. When a day's tour of one island he called Santa María de la Concepción yielded no source of gold, he sailed on to another and another, naming them respectively Fernandina and Isabella. At times he suspected that the seemingly cooperative inhabitants were giving out stories simply to get rid of him. But at other moments he marveled at their willingness to point the way to the precious metal, and wrote confidently, "I cannot fail (with our Lord's help) to find out where it comes from."

All the while, Columbus was making detailed, often rapturous, notes of the flora and fauna. "I saw many trees very unlike ours, and many of them have their branches of different kinds," he wrote. In fact, he added, he even saw one tree with five or six different kinds of branches; "nor are these grafted, for one can say that the grafting is spontaneous." Modern eyes have seen no such polymorphous plant; Columbus had probably seen a tree encased in twining parasites in the lush tropical forest. The fishes he found to be "of the brightest colors in the world, blue, yellow, red and of all colors, and painted in a thousand ways." Land creatures were few, except for parrots and lizards, including some ugly iguanas. He took a certain long-leaved type of vegetation to be a strange variety of *panizo*, a grain-bearing grass common in Spain; he had in fact seen his first maize, or Indian corn. This he had his men gather together with dozens of other samples of leaves, nuts, feathers, twigs and coral to take back to Spain—though he found "the singing of the little birds such that it would seem that man would never wish to leave here."

After a fortnight of exploring the Bahamas, Columbus had no better sense of where Cipangu and Cathay lay than when he had made his first landfall. That these fabled lands were somewhere within the seemingly endless archipelago around him he never doubted for an instant, but in which direction and at what distance he still did not know. Based upon Marco Polo's testimony, however, the mainland should lie considerably farther west than Cipangu; he resolved to find that huge island first.

His guides had frequently indicated that a place they called Colba or Cuba was both wealthy and populous, its harbors, as Columbus put it, "full of ships and sailors both many and great." Grasping with something approaching desperation at the flimsiest of word similarities, Columbus interpreted Colba and Cuba to mean Cipangu. The word "Cubanacan," in reality the islanders' name for a place in the center of the island, became in Columbus' fertile imagination the Great Khan himself. With local pilots and an interpreter aboard, the ships headed southwest to search for Cuba. On October 28 they reached it. Columbus, who had now paid homage to the Savior, the Virgin Mary, Ferdinand and Isabella in naming his islands, christened this one Juana after the Infante Don Juan, the heir apparent. Thus, wrote Ferdinand, his father "aimed to honor both the spiritual and temporal powers."

But once again Columbus found no bustling ports, no sign of high civilization as he expected, only clusters of rude fishermen's huts empty of their occupants. In fact, the only being on hand to note his arrival, Columbus wrote with a hint of wistfulness, was a lone "dog that didn't bark." After a while a few people did appear and approach the explorers. To the question of their king's whereabouts posed with signs and gestures, they responded by pointing up the coast in a westerly direction. Columbus followed the coast west; but he still saw no fine cities. And so with a fresh autumn norther heading the ships, the convoy put about and ran into an inlet now known as Puerto Gibara, where they anchored. Here Columbus decided to probe inland. He chose his Arabic-speaking translator, Luís de Torres, and an old salt named Rodrigo de Jerez, who had once gone to Africa and would presumably know how to treat with a pagan king, and sent them off to look for the Great Khan. While the

Martín Alonso Pinzón, captain of the Pinta on Columbus' first voyage and a prominent shipowner who helped organize the fleet, became the focus after his death in 1493 of an attempt to discredit Columbus. Detractors claimed that Columbus at one point wanted to turn back in mid-Atlantic, but Pinzón forced him to keep going onward, rallying the crews with the cry: "Adelante, Adelante!"—"Sail on! Sail on!"

Vicente Yáñez Pinzón, captain of the Niña and younger brother of Martín Alonso, remained loyal to Columbus during the first voyage and later became justly famous in his own right. In 1500 he sailed southwest to Brazil, then followed the coast northwest to discover the Amazon River, and from there went on to present-day Costa Rica. Eight years later, he sailed again to search for a passage through Central America to the Spice Islands, and this time he is said to have discovered the Yucatan Peninsula and the great Mayan civilization.

scouting party was gone, the rest of the crew amused themselves by teaching the Cubans to say the "Salve" and the "Ave Maria"; and Columbus reassured himself that Cipangu lay just beyond the trees.

He was, of course, destined for disappointment again. When the two emissaries returned on November 5, having gone some 25 miles into the interior, they reported that they had found a village of 1,000 inhabitants but no city, no gold, no spices. Still Columbus could not give up. With his customary optimism he wrote in his journal that the men had found "a great quantity of cotton, and I believe it would sell very well"—but the market he had in mind was the cities of the Great Khan, not those in Spain. The men had also found a curious plant called *tobacos*, which the islanders rolled up and set on fire "to drink the smoke thereof." But Columbus did not foresee the commercial possibilities in that.

Gold was still the thing, and in answer to more urgent questioning, the islanders indicated by word and sign language that at a place to the southeast called Babeque people gathered gold on the beach by candlelight and hammered it into gold bars. Columbus was galvanized into action and set sail at once. But light and contrary winds plagued him in every direction for nine days. Martín Alonso Pinzón, meanwhile, showed his independence once again. Taking advantage of his fast-moving *Pinta*, which could sail in the lightest of winds, Pinzón found it convenient to misread instructions and make directly for Babeque on his own. Columbus was not deceived, and noted Pinzón's departure with displeasure. He put it down to "cupidity," and let the matter drop. Making the best he could of unfavorable circumstances, he detoured with the other two ships to explore the easternmost tip of Cuba.

The detour proved fortunate. He found another island—one of such surpassing beauty that, trying to give an account of it, Columbus ran out of superlatives and wrote that "a thousand tongues would not suffice." The place seemed enchanted. Beyond its broad and sheltered harbor lay lands that were, said Columbus, "beautiful unto admiration." He saw pines and palms, and cultivated fields, and a plain surrounded by mountains—but a plain that "is not completely flat, but is full of smooth and low hills, through which flow many streams of water that fall from these mountains." In a salute to the land of his sovereigns, he called his paradise La Isla Española—Hispaniola in a later currency.

Sadly, Española did not yield the Great Khan of Columbus' dreams, but it soon disclosed a relatively dense population, a more developed culture and economy than the explorers had yet found, and enough gold in evidence to seem promising. Unlike the islanders at San Salvador, who had come out in eager droves at sight of the ships, the people here were elusive, so Columbus sent a party of sailors ashore to capture a few "in order to treat them well and make them lose their fear, that something profitable might be had." The men returned with a naked and very beautiful young woman who, Columbus reported in his journal, appeared rather taken with the Spaniards and in no great hurry to return to her village. Nonetheless, he had her clothed in some of the trade goods and "sent her ashore very honorably."

Just as Columbus had hoped, she rendered such enthusiastic reports of her treatment by the strangers that the explorers were thenceforth re-

The "Niña": a vessel fit for an admiral

On his first Atlantic crossing, Columbus sailed on the *Santa María*, a bulky trading ship with a deplorable tendency to wallow. When she was lost off Hispaniola, he took the smaller *Niña*, which was both stable and nimble.

The *Niña* was a *caravela redonda* (page 49), 70 feet long, with a 23-foot beam and a nine-foot hold that could stow 51 tons of cargo. Her two-and-one-half-inch oak hull planking was fastened with wooden pegs, with the addition of iron bolts at stress points. Vertical skids were fastened to her freeboard in order to protect her plank-

ing while she was careened for repairs.

Her quarter-deck had a small cabin for Columbus. Under the quarter-deck was the helmsman's post, with bunks for the master and pilot built into cabinets barely more than five feet long and 30 inches high, closed by sliding doors. For defense, a small swivel gun firing scrap metal was mounted on the quarter-deck rail, and in the waist was a 3.5-inch cannon firing stoneshot.

Amidships was the wood-burning firebox, and forward, the ship's boat, six sweeps to propel the *Niña* in calms, and spare spars. Arched deck beams

gave the main deck a slight camber, so the crew preferred to sleep on the flat hatch covers; those who could not squeeze in there nestled below.

The bilge water was kept in check by the morning watch, using two wooden pumps amidships. A portable capstan was used to load stores or to weigh anchor. Stability was maintained by shipping ballast and as food stocks were depleted, empty casks were filled with sea water. Stores were packed on loose planks over the bilge and secured by line, leaving narrow walkways for the ship's carpenter.

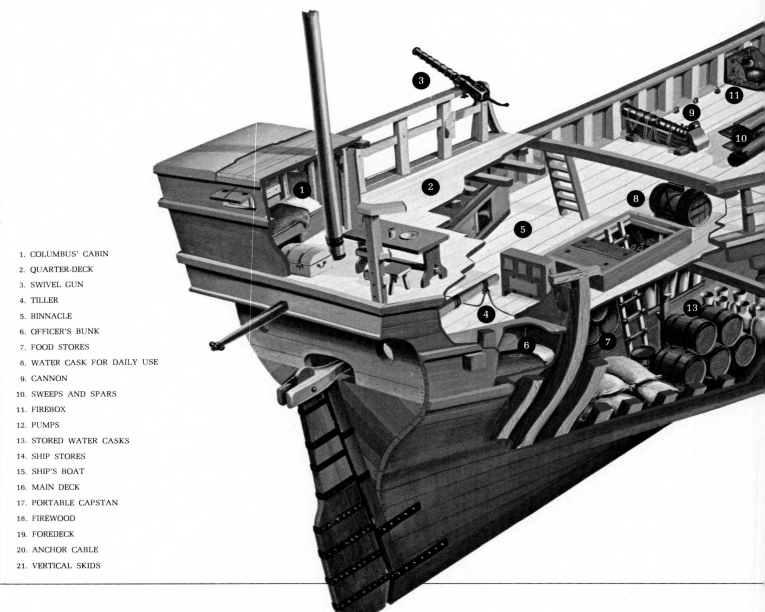

1. COLUMBUS' CABIN
2. QUARTER-DECK
3. SWIVEL GUN
4. TILLER
5. BINNACLE
6. OFFICER'S BUNK
7. FOOD STORES
8. WATER CASK FOR DAILY USE
9. CANNON
10. SWEEPS AND SPARS
11. FIREBOX
12. PUMPS
13. STORED WATER CASKS
14. SHIP STORES
15. SHIP'S BOAT
16. MAIN DECK
17. PORTABLE CAPSTAN
18. FIREWOOD
19. FOREDECK
20. ANCHOR CABLE
21. VERTICAL SKIDS

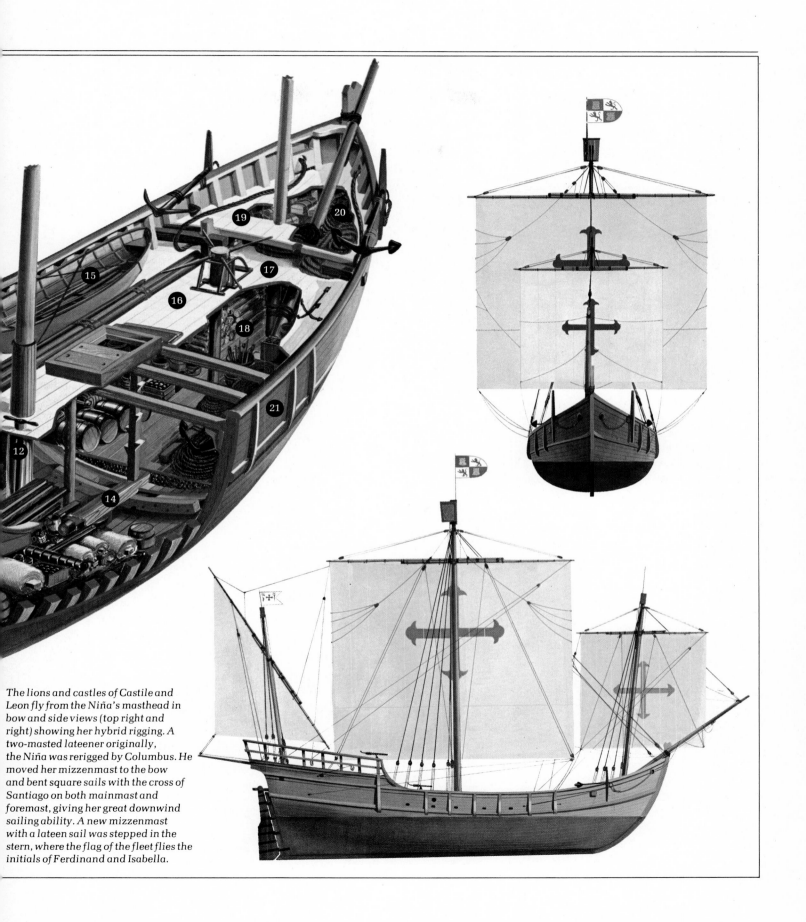

The lions and castles of Castile and Leon fly from the Niña's masthead in bow and side views (top right and right) showing her hybrid rigging. A two-masted lateener originally, the Niña was rerigged by Columbus. He moved her mizzenmast to the bow and bent square sails with the cross of Santiago on both mainmast and foremast, giving her great downwind sailing ability. A new mizzenmast with a lateen sail was stepped in the stern, where the flag of the fleet flies the initials of Ferdinand and Isabella.

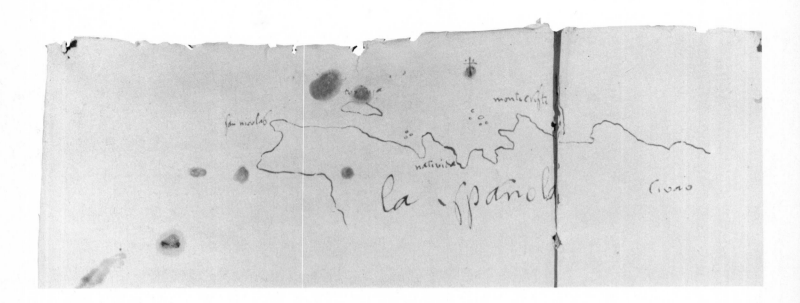

ceived with celebrations everywhere they went. On several occasions chiefs—called caciques in the local language—came out to the *Santa María*. "All these lords are men of few words and fair manners," Columbus wrote in his journal, noting with approval that the chiefs were treated by their people with great reverence. One of them arrived unexpectedly just after the crew had finished dressing ship to mark Annunciation Day. The admiral wrote in his journal, "I was dining at the table below the sterncastle, and at a quick walk he came to sit down beside me, nor would he let me rise to meet him, but begged that I should eat." Columbus ordered a place set for the cacique, and when the meal had ended the chief presented to him a gift of a finely worked belt and a small amount of gold. In return Columbus gave him some red shoes, a bottle of orange-scented cologne, some amber beads and the canopy that hung over the admiral's bed—the cacique had been admiring it. When the pleasant meeting ended, the chief vowed to return soon with more gold and Columbus sent him ashore to a fanfare of cannon salutes.

The chief was as good as his word. Two days later a messenger arrived from one who described himself as the chief of chiefs. The messenger brought an invitation to the strangers to come to the city of this king, named Guacangari, where they would be shown gold and every hospitality. As if to prove the truth of the promise, the messenger presented to Columbus another belt, this one ornamented with red and white fishbones and more gold than Columbus had seen since crossing the Atlantic. When Columbus asked where the gold came from, the messenger repeated what others had said: Cibao. The messenger meant the Cibao region to the southeast, in the island's interior, where small amounts of gold were panned in mountain streams. But Columbus heard what he wished to hear, as he had many times before, and he translated Cibao as Cipangu, his goal. He needed no more assurances. The crew hurried to depart. By sailing east along the coast and then going inland to the south, Columbus was sure they could reach that fabled land by Christmas.

But before he could even clear the coastal waters, he was halted by a

Sketched by Columbus on his first voyage, this map shows the northwest coast of Hispaniola as he traced the shoreline from his landfall at San Nicolás in present-day Haiti eastward to the mountain he named Montecristo in what is now the Dominican Republic. For all his skill at mapmaking, Columbus could not avoid ink blots; the court jester of Charles I joked that Columbus and Egyptian geographer Ptolemy "were twins in the art of blotting."

foolish accident. Perhaps it resulted from the endless celebrations that the islanders had staged the night before as a proper send-off for their friends the Spaniards. But at 11 p.m. on December 24, as the ships drifted about in a windless sea, vigilance aboard the *Santa María* was at low ebb. Columbus, having been awake for 48 hours, went below to sleep. Juan de la Cosa, the ship's captain, was also in his bunk and the helmsman took advantage of the still night air and his officers' absence to turn the tiller over to a cabin boy—something, the journal notes with asperity, Columbus "had always strictly forbidden during the entire voyage, come wind come calm; namely, that they should let a ship's boy steer." The ship was too much for this inexperienced hand. Around midnight the *Santa María* stopped dead in the water. She had nudged her bow onto a coral reef.

Jolted out of his sleep, Columbus rushed up on deck and ordered Juan de la Cosa to take a boat aft and to drop a kedge anchor; he hoped that with fast work the vessel could be pulled free. But de la Cosa and his team panicked, and instead of dropping the kedge they set off as fast as oars would take them for the *Niña*, which had given the reef a wide margin and was safely to windward. To the great credit of Captain Vicente Yáñez Pinzón—brother of Martín Alonso Pinzón, who was still off on his own—he not only refused to permit de la Cosa to board, but sent out a boat of his own to help the beleaguered *Santa María*.

He was too late. Valuable time had been lost and a heavy swell had pushed the *Santa María* hard on the reef, so that the sharp-edged coral was grinding away at her bottom and the ship was starting to come apart at the seams. Desperate, Columbus ordered the mainmast rigging cut to lighten ship, but nothing could save her now. Christmas Day began with the doleful order to abandon ship. Columbus sent a small party ashore to

Fanciful drawings of the New World appeared in this Swiss edition of Columbus' report to his patron, King Ferdinand of Spain, in 1493. At left a nao cruises past an entirely imaginative castle and the islands discovered and named by Columbus; at center, Columbus lands among naked maidens on Insula Hyspana, or Hispaniola; at right is Navidad, the tiny colony that Columbus established on his first voyage.

inform the local chief of the mishap and ask for help. He then told the remaining men to gather all usable gear for transport ashore.

The local cacique was quick to oblige. According to Columbus, he soon appeared weeping in sympathy for the Spaniards' terrible predicament. He brought with him many men and canoes and everyone pitched in to help. Before the day was done, everything of value had been carried to some houses in the chief's compound and there the crew rested.

While Columbus was pondering what to do next, the cacique solved the dilemma; he promised to take Columbus to Cibao in a few days. He also warned Columbus to beware of the Caniba, a fierce people who raided and terrorized the other islands by their custom of eating their victims (whence the word "cannibal"). This was not the first time Columbus had heard of them; the Cubans had spoken of them repeatedly. But Columbus had interpreted all this to suit his own purposes. "Caniba is nothing else than the people of the Grand Khan, which should be very near," he asserted—concluding, since cannibalism was beyond his ken, that "they come to capture the natives, and since the captives don't return they suppose that they've been eaten." Columbus told the cacique that he need not worry, that the Spanish sovereigns would order the Caniba "all brought with their hands bound" and would have them destroyed. To prove his point Columbus had a cannon and musket fired—which caused the terrified Hispaniolans to fall prostrate on the ground.

Recovering from their fright, and anxious to show their gratitude to such a formidable protector, the Hispaniolans produced a costly gesture of their appreciation—"a big mask," Las Casas described it, "that had great pieces of gold in the ears and the eyes and in other parts." The cacique himself made the presentation, bedecking the head of the proud Columbus with a number of other gold ornaments.

This was more like the grandiose wealth and glory that Columbus had come in search of. He recorded that he took such solace from these new events that his grief over the loss of the *Santa María* diminished, and he saw the hand of Providence at work. "In truth," he concluded, the accident "was no disaster but great luck; for it is certain that if I had not run aground, I should have kept to sea without anchoring in this place."

Suddenly his course was clear. He would build a fortress and leave a party of 39 men behind while he and the rest sailed home aboard the surviving *Niña* to report on what they had found—and then prepare an even larger second voyage. "They shall have boards of which to build the whole fortress"—a reference to the wood salvaged from the *Santa María*—"and provisions for bread and wine for more than a year, and seeds to sow, and the ship's barge, and a caulker, a carpenter, a gunner and a cooper." In remembrance of the Christmas accident that seemed to have put them there miraculously, he named the fort Navidad. Having thus founded the first colony of Europeans in the New World, he set sail on January 4, 1493—beginning the New Year homeward bound.

He was only two days out when a familiar form loomed up on the horizon; it was the *Pinta*. When she caught up with the *Niña*, Martín Alonso Pinzón hurried over to explain his absence, alleging that he had lost Columbus "against his will." Columbus was angry enough to note in his diary that he "knew not whence came the insolence and disloyalty"

In his cryptic signature, Columbus demonstrates his sense of divine mission. The Greco-Latin cipher includes his name, spelled with an X or Greek letter chi as XpoFERENS—pronounced Christoferens—the Christ Bearer. Historians believe the initials above the name in Latin stand for "Servant am I of the Most High Saviour, Christ Son of Mary."

Granted to him as Admiral of the Ocean Sea by the Spanish sovereigns, Columbus' coat of arms contains castle and lion, signets of the kingdoms of Castile and León, anchors symbolizing the admiral's title, and to the left of them, islands of the New World he discovered. At the bottom is Columbus' personal emblem.

of this troublesome fellow—but practical enough to be glad of company. Pinzón had found no gold, and Columbus let the matter pass.

On the homeward passage Columbus faced a new set of problems; he now had to contend with the prevailing easterlies that had blown him across the Atlantic four months before. To try to retrace his ships' journey by sailing into the teeth of these winds would have been foolhardy, if not impossible. Yet Columbus was well aware of the prevailing westerlies that in winter buffeted Portugal's Atlantic coast 800 miles north of the Canaries. Intuitively he gambled that those winds might just extend clear across the Atlantic. With that in mind his strategy was to work north and east close-hauled on the starboard tack until he reached the latitude of the Portuguese coast. Then, if all went well, Columbus could sail home on the generous shoulders of following winds.

This strategy took him on the best eastward route across the Atlantic in winter. For two weeks the caravels clawed up the wind, altering course from north-by-east to north-northeast to northeast as the wind hauled around to the west. Several times the *Niña* had to round up into the wind to wait for the *Pinta*; the ship that had been so swift on the outward passage now sailed poorly close-hauled because her mizzen had been damaged. "If her captain, Martín Alonso Pinzón, had taken as much care to provide a good mast in the Indies, where there were so many," Columbus wrote testily, "as he was greedy to fill up the ship with gold, he would have done well." However, by February 4 the fleet had come far enough for Columbus to order the second leg of his course—due east.

With the weather turning cold and blustery, the *Niña* raced along at high speed, making the best time of the entire voyage. On February 6 she put 200 nautical miles behind her, some of that time at speeds of 11 knots. But trouble was ahead; on February 12, as the ships neared the Azores, they began to run into tempestuous weather. Gale winds raged out of the southwest to send seas crashing over the decks, nearly overwhelming the tiny ships. To make matters worse, they were light on ballast; they had used up most of their provisions, wine and water. Aboard the *Niña*, Columbus met that crisis by filling the water and wine pipes with sea water. Meanwhile, he tried to keep in touch with his errant comrade. All through the night of February 13 he lit flares from the *Niña*, and Martín Alonso Pinzón answered from the *Pinta*. But the answering flares ceased, and Columbus feared the *Pinta* had gone down.

Death seemed close at hand for the *Niña*, too, and the crew began to say their prayers with mounting dread. Someone suggested making a vow to go on a pilgrimage—walking all the way to Our Lady of Guadalupe if they were saved—and they drew lots to see who should go. Columbus ordered a hatful of chick-peas—one pea for every man aboard the ship, and a single pea to be marked with a cross. Putting in his own hand first, Columbus drew out the marked pea himself, and so the lot fell on him. As the storm continued, the men made still more vows and drew more lots. Finally, when nothing seemed to appease the elements, they decided that if they lived the whole company should go shirtless to the first shrine of the Virgin they came to.

Columbus related that in desperation he wrote on a separate parchment a detailed account of what he had discovered, wrapped it in a waxed cloth and attached a written promise of 1,000 ducats to the finder who should deliver it to the King and Queen of Spain. Then he sealed the lot in a barrel. Wary of adding to the terrors that already gripped the crew, he told no one what it was; hoping that they would suppose it to be some further act of devotion to the heavens, he then consigned the barrel to the furious sea. So far as is known, it was never found.

By the end of the next day, the anguished crew had reason to feel their prayers had been answered. The winds and waves began to subside. For four days they had rough sailing, but on February 18 the *Niña* was safe in the harbor of Santa María in the Azores. Here, 800 miles from the European mainland, the ship was revictualed and the crew went ashore to seek a shrine where they could carry out their pilgrimage vows.

Then they put to sea again. Two weeks later, on the night of March 4, rushing headlong under poles bared by yet another storm, they spotted the rocky cliffs of the Portuguese coast by moonlight. By morning the

A desperate last gamble for glory

At the tragic end of his third voyage, Columbus (right foreground) is clapped in irons for having misruled Hispaniola.

Niña was nearing the Tagus' broad mouth. Columbus had, of course, been intending to go to Spain; but with his sails in tatters and his ship near collapse, he had no choice but to call at the first port he reached. So he dropped anchor near Restello, about four miles from Lisbon.

His arrival stunned the Portuguese. Even before the nature of the voyage was known, the bedraggled ship and crew caused a sensation, because the recent storms—the worst in memory—had wrought such havoc all along the coast. Some 25 merchant vessels had been lost during the winter, and others had been lying in port for four months without being able to get out. "The townspeople spent all that morning saying prayers" for Columbus and his crew, Las Casas wrote, "and after he had got in, the people came to see them for wonder at how they escaped."

Columbus had reason to fear the official reaction, considering the rivalry between Spain and Portugal. He wrote at once to João II, explaining where he had been and asking permission to repair his ships. Four

---

Of Columbus' three later journeys to the New World—all of which ended in failure, frustration and even disgrace—none was more harrowing or heroic than the great explorer's fourth and final passage. It was a supreme triumph of will and seamanship. Indeed, Columbus himself termed it his "High Voyage," *El Alto Viaje.*

After being sent back in chains from Hispaniola in 1500 for failing to quell civil unrest on the island, Columbus was desperate to regain his lost grace. At 51, he was an old man afflicted with arthritis, but he pleaded with Ferdinand and Isabella for a last chance to find a passage to India. Eager to be rid of him, the monarchs authorized a fleet of four caravels and sent him off.

Columbus was able to reach the Caribbean just ahead of a gathering hurricane. Rushing to Hispaniola, from which he had been barred by royal edict, he sent ashore warnings of the impending storm. The new governor sneered at the alarm; soon afterward he dispatched a treasure fleet, most of which was lost in the hurricane.

Columbus weathered the storm in a Hispaniolan cove. When the hurricane was over, he sailed to Honduras to search for a passage to India. He decided to beat east along the coast, fighting strong winds and currents. Had he gone west to Yucatan, he might have found the great Mayan civilization.

As it was, the fleet battled the relentless wind for 28 days, tacking back and forth, ending many a day still within sight of landmarks spied at dawn. "It was one continual rain, thunder and lightning," Columbus reported. "The ships lay exposed to the weather, with sails torn, and anchors, rigging, cables, boats and many of the stores lost; the people, exhausted and so down in the mouth that they were all the time making vows to be good, to go on pilgrimages and all that; yea, even hearing one another's confessions! Other tempests I have seen, but none that lasted so long or so grim as this."

At last the coast turned south and the fleet was able to sail with the fierce winds abeam. For eight months Columbus sailed the coast to Panama, probing bays and rivers, fighting Indians—and hearing of a great sea across a narrow isthmus. Columbus thought the land neck could only be the Malay Peninsula. His arthritis was crippling, his eyes were inflamed and he came down with malarial fevers. His crews had suffered deprivation, drowning and despair. His ships were riddled by teredo worms. Columbus turned back.

One caravel was abandoned to hostile Indians; another worm-eaten hulk was left in Panama. After a desperate race to Jamaica, decks awash, Columbus beached his ships. Living in huts on deck, the marooned men waited while 14 of their fellows canoed across the 108-mile channel to Hispaniola.

But for seven long months the new governor of Hispaniola refused to let Columbus be rescued. Starving, the explorer warned local Indian chiefs that because they had refused to provide food, God would show his wrath. His almanac predicted a lunar eclipse on the last night of February 1504. When it began, the Indians wailed in terror. Columbus exacted a promise of food in return for the moon.

It was August before a rescue ship arrived. Now broken in spirit and in body, Columbus returned to Spain, only to find Queen Isabella, his patron, dying. His own life—a High Voyage from start to finish—was at its end; he died in Valladolid on May 20, 1506, barely seven months after his return.

days later the answer arrived from João—Columbus could dock and repair his ship in Lisbon, and he was cordially summoned to the royal presence; a nobleman was assigned to conduct him there.

King João treated Columbus politely, commanding his courtiers to give the explorer whatever he wished—despite the fact that, having turned down Columbus' proposal some eight years before, he suffered a certain chagrin. Columbus for his part was not in the least generous in triumph; the Portuguese chroniclers noted that in telling his tale "he always exceeded the bounds of truth and made the story of gold, silver and riches much greater than it was"—though there was no way they could know whether or not he was exaggerating. The courtiers present grew so agitated at Columbus' braggadocio that they urged the King to have the insolent man killed—noting that, "inasmuch as he was discourteous and elated they could fix it so that any one of his shortcomings could seem to be the true cause of his death." But this the King declined to do. "Like the God-fearing prince that he was," the chroniclers recorded, João "on the contrary showed him honor and much kindness and therewith sent him away." With his men refreshed and the *Niña* overhauled, Columbus sailed on to Palos—the Spanish port from which he had embarked seven months and 12 days before. He reached there on March 15—the first of the great Renaissance explorers to sail to the western shores of the Atlantic, and return.

The peripatetic Martín Alonso Pinzón turned up on the very same tide, bringing the *Pinta* into Palos harbor within hours of the *Niña*'s arrival. When separated from Columbus in the February 13 storm, Pinzón had been blown clear past the Azores, made landfall at Vigo on the northwestern coast of Spain, and then swung back south to put in at Palos. Pinzón had supposed that Columbus' ship had sunk, that he, Pinzón, and his own crew were the only survivors, and that he would be able to present his side of the story to the Spanish monarchs. Finding the *Niña* already at anchor, he had only to look forward to inevitable charges of insubordination. The shock, following the physical strain of the return voyage, was too much; within the month Pinzón was dead.

Columbus proceeded to a triumphant welcome. He sent a messenger to the King and Queen, now holding court in Barcelona, 800 miles across the country, and soon received an encouraging reply—addressed to "Don Christopher Columbus, our Admiral of the Ocean Sea, Viceroy and Governor of the Islands that he hath discovered in the Indies." This was an auspicious start; the titles of nobility he had demanded were now his without question. "We have taken much pleasure in learning whereof you write, and that God gave so good a result to your labors," they went on, "and we desire that you come here forthwith." Columbus wasted no time. He outfitted himself with fine clothes suitable to a Spanish grandee and set forth with an entourage made up of several of his crew, 40 parrots and other brightly colored birds, and six captive Indians.

When Columbus arrived in Barcelona, "All the court and the city came out to meet him," Ferdinand later wrote, "and the Catholic sovereigns received him in public, seated with all majesty and grandeur on rich thrones under a canopy of cloth of gold." When the returning hero knelt before them in a ritual of knightly obeisance, they rose to greet him, a singular tribute seldom extended by royalty to a common man. They then bade him rise himself, proffering a chair of honor on Isabella's right hand. After inspecting the gold and the Indians he had brought back, they told Columbus that the Crown was prepared to send another voyage as soon as he could make ready—and the whole assemblage repaired to the royal chapel for heartfelt prayers of thanksgiving.

In years to come, his triumphal welcome would seem to Columbus all too brief and meager a reward. He would continue to make discoveries in three subsequent voyages—planting the flag of Spain on the Leeward Islands, the Virgin Islands and Puerto Rico on the second, beginning in September 1493; Trinidad and the mouth of the Orinoco River in Venezuela on the third in 1498; Honduras and Panama on the fourth in 1502. But trouble would dog his every step.

He found on making his second voyage that the men who had stayed behind at Navidad had been killed by angry Hispaniolans before they could discover the source of the island's gold; spending a year and a half in an ill-fated effort to found another colony, Columbus returned home to Spain for more men and supplies. The "colonizers" who vied for the chance to go on his third voyage were in reality adventurers after gold; they refused to cooperate in establishing a colony or in tending the crops and livestock necessary to their survival. When the gold did not materialize, they rebelled and tried to kill him; Columbus responded by hanging the ringleaders. When some of the surviving malcontents sailed home on their own and word of Columbus' difficulties reached the Court, even his royal patrons turned against him. They stripped him of the title of governor, which his contract had granted in perpetuity, and sent a replacement who went so far as to ship the astonished Columbus and his kin home in chains. Yielding to his importunings, Ferdinand and Isabella allowed him to make a fourth voyage in 1502. But that trip, although a triumph of navigation, reaped him no rewards. He was beset by Indian attacks (pages 76-77), by desertions from among his crew and by sickness. In 1504 he sailed home to die.

That was the sad end to Columbus' life as an explorer. He never found the Cathay he had sought so long. But he had sailed 3,000 miles across an uncharted sea, and back again; he had given Spain an empire covering one third of the Western Hemisphere—and he had prepared Europe for the circumnavigation of the world in a later era. Half a century after his time, the Spanish chronicler Francisco López de Gómera was to write that Columbus' first voyage was the "greatest event since the creation of the world (excluding the incarnation and death of Him who created it)." But Columbus would enjoy no such acclaim in his own time. Scarcely a decade after his epic feat, he was obsessed with the idea that enemies were everywhere, and bereft of the ebullient optimism that had for so long carried him over the shoals of hard times. A letter he wrote to his elder son, Diego, shortly before his death on May 20, 1506, suggests his mixture of self-pity and righteousness: "I have served their Highnesses with as great diligence and love as I might have employed to win paradise and more; and if somewhere I have been wanting, that was impossible, or much beyond my knowledge and strength. Our Lord God in such cases asketh nothing more of man than good will."

Gold brought back by Columbus from the New World forms the core of this spectacular 16th Century monstrance in the great cathedral of Toledo, Spain. During the feast of Corpus Christi each spring, a consecrated wafer, or Host, is placed inside. The German goldsmith Henry Arfe shaped the elaborate six-foot masterpiece out of various precious gems and enamels, carved silver filigree and 35 pounds of gold.

A natural kingdom to enrapture the senses

Among the most rapturous entries in the journals of Columbus are the accounts of the exotic plants and animals found on his four voyages to the New World. No detail was spared in describing the new and wondrously exciting tropical flora and fauna of the islands and mainland.

Much of what the explorers saw was so alien to their experience that they struggled to find comparisons. The trunkfish, for example, was likened to a pig and the sea cow to a mermaid. One tree never successfully identified was said to "make a fruit nine inches around and flat as a pancake. It has the skin of a chestnut, is full inside like an egg and has the flavor of acorns."

The journals told of astonishing sights: "tortoises as large as a wooden shield," "reptiles weighing 15 to 20 pounds," "trees that seem to touch the sky." The marvels were so plentiful that Columbus swore "a thousand tongues would not suffice" to tell of them all.

Columbus took great care to store away samples of new specimens so that his royal patrons might bear witness to the unbelievable. Yet it was not until the Englishman John White crossed the Atlantic nearly 100 years later and returned with field sketches—from which these meticulously detailed watercolors were made—that Europeans could see what the plants and animals of the Americas looked like.

Common to the tropical western Atlantic, this dusky-plumaged sea bird, the booby, put on a show for Columbus' crews with its habit of diving headlong into the ocean for food. Erroneously believing that "these birds sleep ashore and go to sea mornings," Columbus thought they were sure signs of land.

The frigate, or man-of-war bird, with its seven-foot wingspan and forked tail, was a common sight in American tropical waters. Columbus made careful note of its piratical nature; these birds, he said, swooped down to make the boobies "vomit what they have eaten, in order to eat it, and live on nothing else."

Its long, graceful neck, extraordinary bill and exquisite coloring made the flamingo an awesome sight. Though flamingos were known from southern Europe, the European species was largely white bodied, nothing like the birds found on the islands off Cuba.

A Flamingo.

60

The prickly skin and sharp, saw-toothed tuft of the pineapple did not keep the curious Columbus from sampling its sweet meat. He described the fruit, which he found in Caribbean islands growing on shrublike stalks, as being "in the shape of a pine cone, twice as big, which fruit is excellent and can be cut with a knife like a turnip and seems very wholesome."
In Guadeloupe, Columbus found that the islanders made wine from pineapple juice.

The Pyne frute .

This globular fruit called mammee by the Caribbean islanders seemed to the Spaniards to incorporate the characteristics of half a dozen Europec varieties. "They are fruits that grow on very tall trees like cedars," wrote one seaman, "and are like big lemons. Eacl has two, three or four stones like nuts. 1 skin is like the pomegranate and it tastes like a peach or a good pear."

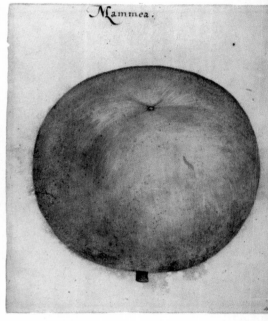

Mammea .

Thought at first to be "the same as the crocodiles of the Nile," the huge reptile seen by Columbus on the coast of Panama was probably this North American alligator. These animals "go ashore to stay and sleep and spread an odor as if all the musk in the world were there. They are so carnivorous and cruel that if they catch a man sleeping ashore they drag him to the water to devour him, though they are timid and flee when attacked."

Allagatto . This being but one moneth old was 3 . foote 4 . ynches in length . and lyue in water.

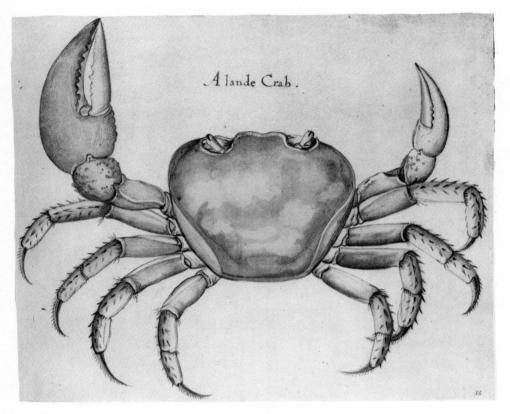

A lande Crab.

With their oversized pincer and popping eyes, land crabs such as this 10.5-inch specimen were an impressive sight to the Spaniards, who found swarms of the creatures along the coast of Cuba. Columbus mentions seeing them, but makes no reference to eating these "enormous crabs" although they were a staple of local Caribbean diet.

This large, swift-moving lizard, called an iguana by Caribbean islanders, filled Columbus and his men with awe. "It is seven palms in length," wrote Columbus, indicating a measure equal to 56 inches, "and I believe there are many like it in these islands." Although the explorers believed the reptile to be a man-eater, they sampled its meat. Roasting the iguana between two pieces of wood, they pronounced the creature to be "very good," with "very white" flesh.

Igwano. Some of thes are 3. fote in length. and lyue on land.

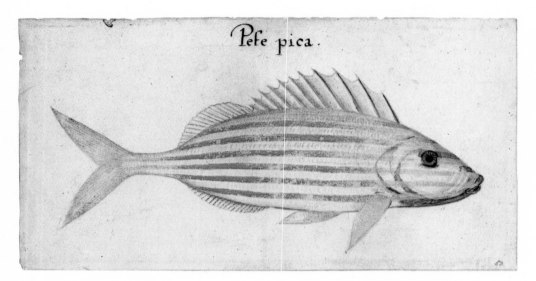

Pefe pica.

Garopa.

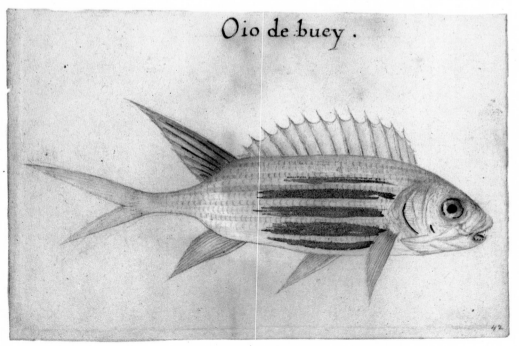

Oio de buey.

The striped grunt (labeled here Pefe pica), speckled grouper (Garopa) and long-finned soldierfish (Oio de buey) were among the swarms of tropical fishes that captivated Columbus. There were species familiar to Spaniards in the waters of the Caribbean—hake, sole, skate and pompano—but many were "so unlike ours and the colors so bright that there is no man who would not marvel and would not take great delight in seeing them." The abundance was of equal wonderment to the observant admiral, for "the sea seemed choked with tunnyfish."

Expansive forefins creating a wondrous cross between bird and fish, the flying fish, called volador (labeled here Bolador) in Spanish, was frequently sighted planing from wave to wave and riding strong breezes to heights of 20 feet before alighting on the decks of Columbus' vessels.

Bolador.

The flyeng fishe.

Chapter 3

East from Portugal to an empire of spices

A fleet of Portuguese carracks, work-horse vessels of 16th Century exploration, sails up the Tagus River to Lisbon in this contemporary painting.

hortly before noon on Saturday, July 8, 1497, all Lisbon reverberated to the tread of a great procession that prayerfully wended its way to the harbor, where Portugal's newest carracks rode to anchor with pennants flying. Half a dozen chroniclers immortalized the day in prose and verse. They recounted how rank after rank passed down to the quays: red-robed bishops, black-frocked priests, tonsured friars, nobles in court regalia, ships' captains and liveried seamen. Towering over the assemblage from his mount on horseback rode the stout figure of Captain Major Vasco da Gama, who was about to launch diminutive Portugal on the greatest maritime venture in all her long seafaring history.

On commission from Manuel I, da Gama was taking a fleet of four vessels on an unprecedented 27,000-mile round-trip voyage to far-off India along a route around Africa proved possible by Bartolomeu Dias. In more than half a century of energetic exploration, nothing approaching the epic proportions of this voyage had even been considered.

In the awe-struck crowds that gathered along the route to watch kin, friends and their leaders depart, a plaintive note was sounded amid the chanted prayers and trumpets. "The wails of women sadden'd all the coast," wrote Portugal's poet Luis de Camões in lyric remembrance, adding that little children, imitating their elders, "lament for sorrows deeper than they know." Women and children were not the only onlookers gripped with emotion and dread. "See whither covetousness and ambition are carrying away these wretched men!" murmured some masculine voices, according to the chronicler Jeronymo Osorio. "Would it not have been far more tolerable to be carried off by any kind of death onshore, rather than to be buried in the sea waves so far from home?"

Foreboding and lamentations notwithstanding, the thrill of high expectation carried the day. At his mountain castle outside the city, King Manuel had granted da Gama a private audience, had given him a consecrated silk banner emblazoned with the Cross of the Order of Christ and had promised liberal earthly rewards all around. A papal bull accorded eternal salvation to all those fearless souls taking part in the adventure. At the waterfront the priest of the local chapel said Mass, invoking the blessings of the Almighty. At last the intrepid seafarers boarded their craft and, to a salute of booming cannon, the ships laboriously weighed anchor and filed down the Tagus River, bound for India.

Ten years had passed since da Gama's heroic predecessor, Bartolomeu Dias, had set out on the journey that took him around the Cape of Good Hope. Since his return with the news that the sea route to the Indian Ocean had been found at last, no new voyages of exploration had been dispatched to the Eastern Seas. But Portugal had not been idle during these years. She had used the time for gathering information, for planning strategy and negotiating with her growing rival, Spain.

First chronologically, and high in importance, was the need for information. Though Dias had demonstrated that the two great known oceans of the world—the Atlantic and the Indian—were connected, he had brought back no information on what conditions might be expected along the northeast African coast and in Indian waters. For that intelli-

Although he stood on the shoulders of giants of discovery like Henry the Navigator and João II who preceded him, King Manuel I, portrayed above in a decorative letter from an illuminated manuscript, presided over Portugal's finest hour. While he was king from 1495 to 1521, his nation dominated the sea-lanes between Europe and Asia, discovered Brazil, made its first contact with China and became a colonial power in India.

gence the Portuguese anxiously awaited the report of a second explorer.

In 1487, the same year Dias had set out down the African coast, the then-reigning monarch, João II, had prudently dispatched Pero da Covilhã on a complementary mission to India via an overland route. Covilhã seems to have been blessed with an ear for language, an eye for mannerism and a knack for disguise; so fluent was his Arabic that he could pass among the Arabs themselves without detection. He had already put that fluency to the test as a spy for Portugal in Morocco.

Covilhã set out for India by way of Barcelona. He proceeded to Naples, Rhodes, Alexandria and Cairo, where he arrived with a pocketful of letters of credit. Wearing Arab garb and posing as a merchant, he then joined a caravan that successfully carried him through the Moslem heartland as far as Aden, at the foot of the Red Sea. There he boarded a ship and sailed east to Calicut, a major Indian port on the Malabar Coast. Here, at the vital nexus of the Oriental spice market—where Eastern and Western trade routes met, where not only spices but gold, precious stones and grain changed hands—Pero da Covilhã got down to the serious business of his mission, reconnoitering the lay of the land.

Still posing as an Arab, he visited port after port, going north along the Indian coast as far as Goa. Next he boarded an Arab ship and crossed westward again to East Africa and worked his way down the other shore of the Indian Ocean, calling at the thriving ports of Malindi, Mombasa, Mozambique and Sofala, on the southeast coast of Africa. He then returned to Cairo, arriving in 1490, three years after setting out from home.

Pero da Covilhã had spent his time profitably. He had traveled up and down both shores of the Indian Ocean, nosing his way in and out of half a dozen vital ports. He had learned which commodities came from where; that pepper and ginger were grown in India; that cloves and cinnamon were brought there by Moslem sailors from islands to the east; that gold came from the African interior to Sofala, whence it was shipped overseas. He had learned the routes the Moslems followed and the schedules they kept—timing their arrivals at and departures from the Indian Ocean ports in August and February to make the most of the monsoon winds.

With all this invaluable information up his ample sleeves, Covilhã intended to proceed from Cairo back to Portugal. But in Cairo he was contacted by two messengers from King João: he was to turn south again and resume the search for the Christian kingdom of Prester John, thought to exist somewhere in inland Africa (*pages 34-35*). Covilhã never found it. Nor did he ever return to Portugal; reaching Ethiopia, he found instead a congenial place for himself as the trusted but captive adviser to the reigning king, and in that court passed his remaining years.

No report of Pero da Covilhã's journey has ever been found. But it is reasonable, given Covilhã's fidelity, to believe that one existed and that it was returned to Lisbon through the offices of the messengers who had located him in Cairo in 1490. The report would have given the Portuguese information about all but 1,000 miles of the East African coast—between the Keiskama River, the site just north of the cape where Dias had turned back, and Sofala, the southern limit of Covilhã's journey.

Covilhã's information would also, however, have reached Europe at more or less the same time as some other, not so welcome, information:

that Christopher Columbus, sailing under the flag of rival Spain, had successfully voyaged west across the vast Atlantic, and discovered land that he asserted was the Orient.

With Spain and Portugal both vying now for trade with the Orient, Pope Alexander VI stepped in on the side of Spain. On May 4, 1493, he issued the *Inter caetera,* a bull in which he granted Spain exclusive rights to trade in and possess forever all lands west of an imaginary line running down the Atlantic Ocean approximately 350 miles west of the Portuguese-held Cape Verde Islands.

But João objected to the terms of the bull. He was willing enough to let Spain have her discoveries in the West—there was as yet no proof that they were the "Indies," as Columbus called them, nor any proof of real riches in them. But João was determined to keep the Spanish as far away from Africa as possible. He sent emissaries to meet with Spanish representatives at Tordesillas, a town in northwest Spain near the border between the two countries, and there they negotiated for a year. The Treaty of Tordesillas, signed in June 1494, settled the matter. It represented a coup for Portugal. By its terms, the imaginary line was moved some 950 miles farther west—nearly three times the distance of the original proposal. It not only preserved the existing Portuguese monopoly along the African coast, but preserved Portuguese access to the eastern sea route—and to cities already known to exist in the real India.

João died a year and a half later of dropsy. He was succeeded by his 26-year-old cousin, Manuel I, who profited enormously from João's prudent forethought and shrewd strategy.

By 1495, when Manuel took over, the Portuguese had every reason for confidence in resuming voyages to the East. They also had every reason for confidence in the fleet they assembled to sail it.

The fleet consisted of four ships, two specially built for this voyage and all four meticulously fitted out under the experienced eye of that earlier explorer, Bartolomeu Dias. The first two were sturdy naos, square rigged on two masts and with a triangular lateen sail on the mizzen. The Portuguese christened them the *São Gabriel* and the *São Rafael,* for the angels of glad tidings and companionship, and armed them with 20 guns. The third vessel was the *Berrio,* a smaller lateen-rigged caravel of about 100 tons bought from a Portuguese merchant and meant for swift sailing and inshore scouting along the African coast.

The last vessel was an unnamed storeship of about 300 tons. According to the chronicler Lopes de Castanheda, her spacious hold allowed for generous provisions that included daily rations per man of a pound of salt beef, one and a half pounds of biscuits, two and a half pints of water and one and a quarter pints of wine. There were also lentils, sardines, plums, almonds, onions, garlic, mustard, salt, sugar and honey for all—in quantities judged to be a three-year supply. In addition to the provisions for the voyagers themselves, the ships carried a store of caps, glass beads, copper bowls, little round bells and tin rings to be given to such rulers as they might encounter, and a cargo of striped cotton cloth, olive oil, sugar and coral with which they intended to trade for spices.

In selecting a leader for the expedition, King Manuel I had proceeded with care. The voyage was to be of extraordinary length; its captain must therefore have personal endurance and resolution in the face of discontent. The venture was also to be so costly that the Crown needed both the capital and the political support that only the nobles of the land could supply. And that called for an expedition leader from their own ranks.

The 37-year-old da Gama, whose background was impeccable, and whose piercing eyes conveyed a steely will beyond mere breeding, met the requirements admirably. Da Gama was born in 1460, the year that Henry the Navigator died. His birthplace was the coastal town of Sines, midway between Lisbon and Cape St. Vincent. Vasco, the youngest of three sons, belonged to the seventh generation of a family with a proud military tradition; they descended from one Alvaro Annes da Gama, who had helped oust the last Moors from the Algarve in 1238. Vasco's father, Estevão, was civil governor of Sines; and Vasco himself had served with distinction during the reign of João II in Portugal's 1483 war against Castile. But Vasco's talents were not merely military; he had studied the exciting new science of navigation and had been trained in astronomy, probably by Abraham Zacuto ben Samuel, the learned Hebrew who was astronomer royal to João II.

Da Gama was a difficult man—arrogant and sometimes cruel. He once extorted information from a captive by pouring boiling oil on his naked belly. But he could as easily be moved to compassion; he had an abiding affection for his brother Paulo and he dealt fairly with his men. When he required them to learn to be carpenters, ropemakers, caulkers and blacksmiths—the better to take care of themselves when far from home— he increased their pay from five crusadoes a month to seven. Most important, he combined firmness of will with a quickness of intellect that would serve him brilliantly on the voyage ahead.

As captain major, or fleet commander, Vasco da Gama sailed in the new nao *São Gabriel,* with Gonçalo Alvares as his captain. He appointed his brother Paulo captain of the *São Rafael.* Nicolau Coelho, an experienced mariner, was to command the swift caravel *Berrio,* and the storeship went to Gonçalo Nunes, one of his personal retainers. Several of his other officers were seasoned explorers who had been to the cape with Dias. Among the 170 officers and men were pursers, petty officers, men-at-arms, gunners, musicians, a couple of men who could speak Arabic, and others who could interpret African dialects—and an anonymous diarist who left the only eyewitness account of the voyage.

Leaving Lisbon on that epochal day in July, da Gama and his fleet sailed down the Moroccan coast, past the Canary Islands and on to the Cape Verdes, 425 miles seaward of the West African bulge. At the islands, they put in for fresh food and water and made some minor repairs to their ships. They were under way again on August 3—and well started on one of the most brilliant excursions in maritime history.

Instead of retracing the wakes of his predecessors, who had sailed east from the Cape Verdes to follow the general contours of the African coast, da Gama took his fleet on a bold and imaginative course west-southwest, heading into the broad Atlantic. No one knows exactly why he chose this course, but it is likely that he had consulted with Dias on plans for the

The newborn art of navigation

Centuries before the invention of the essential instruments of celestial navigation—the compass, astrolabe (*right*), sextant and chronometer—Mediterranean mariners sailed their craft out of sight of land, by day and by night, using as their guide an untidy amalgam of sea lore, common sense and a few basic astronomical observations.

They knew that the sun came up in the east and set in the west and that by night certain stars did the same. To the north, the Great Bear wheeled overhead, serving as both a directional beacon and a crude timepiece. Early navigators also used winds, currents, water depths and even the migratory habits of birds to determine their position.

But not until the 11th Century did a device come into use aboard ship that could at any hour, in darkness or light,

in fair weather or foul, give a mariner his direction of sail with reasonable accuracy. This tool was the magnetic compass, whose pointer constantly indicated the magnetic North Pole.

The first marine compasses were crude in the extreme: simply an iron needle that had been magnetized by rubbing against a piece of magnetite and then floated on a wood chip in a bowl of water. Later came a more sophisticated design in which a circular card marked with points of the compass was attached to the needle; the whole affair then rotated on a brass pin in the bottom of an empty cup.

The compass was a boon beyond price to the navigator. But for all its virtues, it still remained true that the compass could only point direction. Exact location remained a mystery.

The navigator practiced around the clock, a point emphasized in this 16th Century woodcut showing two oversized navigators sighting the sun with an astrolabe (right), and a star with a cross-staff (left).

Fitted snugly in its ivory case, this 16th Century Italian compass is typical of the type taken on the voyages of discovery. The fleur-de-lis emblem that marks north— still common on modern compasses— is an embellishment of the letter T, which stands for "tramontana," literally the Italian name for the north wind.

Reading the map in the sky

By the time European mariners sailed forth into the trackless oceans in the 15th Century, they had a second vital navigational aid. This was a rudimentary sort of celestial navigation called latitude sailing, by which they could determine their position north or south of the equator.

The ancient Greeks had figured out the principle of latitude, but it took Portugal's Prince Henry the Navigator and his cosmologists to retool this arcane theory into a seaworthy technology. Its success depended on measuring the angle between the observer's horizon and a celestial body—usually the sun at its zenith, or the polestar.

With this angle established, the navigator went to tables called an ephemeris and read on what parallel of latitude he would have to be for the sun or star to be seen at that altitude on that day. With a sighting taken on a calm sea, exact latitude could be calculated. But to determine where he was, an explorer also had to know his longitude —how far east or west he had sailed— and that was a different matter.

Descended from the far more complex instrument of Arabian astronomy, this 16th Century brass astrolabe was suspended from a cord, to hang perpendicular to sea level, while the sun or a star was sighted through two small holes in the plates on its movable vane. The altitude of the celestial body then could be read from the graduated scale around the rim.

With one end of this cross-staff held to his eye and the other end pointed toward the sun or star, the navigator attached a transom piece to the shaft (four choices are shown at right, one of them attached) and adjusted it to fit exactly between the heavenly body and the horizon. The angle of altitude was then read on the shaft.

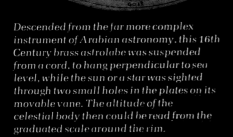

The earliest of the instruments that navigators used to measure altitude, the seaman's quadrant was so simple in design that a navigator could easily make one for himself if necessary. Essentially a quarter circle cut from wood or brass, the quadrant was held vertically by one person who lined up the sun or a star through the sights along an edge while another person read the altitude—usually inaccurate—indicated by the plumb line.

To save himself hours of tedious calculations, the early navigator used sea tables called an ephemeris in which the declination (altitude at the equator) of various heavenly bodies had already been figured out for all the days of the year. Latitude was established simply by subtracting this figure from another obtained by observing the local altitude of the same heavenly body. The page below is from astronomer Pedro Medina's navigational manual Arte de Navegar.

With a nocturnal, the time of night was calculated by marking the progress of certain stars that traced out small circles around the polestar every 24 hours. The polestar was sighted through the center aperture of the nocturnal, and the long arm was pivoted to touch a circling star. The time was found on the hour dial, notched to be read by feel at night.

Declinacion del sol.

Año. Primero.

Octubre.			Nouiéb.			Diziébre.		
dias	B.	M.	dias	B.	M.	dias	B.	M.
1	vi.	l vi.	1	x vii.	xx ix.	1	xx iiij.	vii.
2	vii.	x ix.	2	x vii.	xl v.	2	xx iij.	x j.
3	vii.	xl i.	3	x viij.	ti.	3	xx iij.	xx.
4	viii.	iiii.	4	x viij.	x viii.	4	xx iij.	xx.
5	viii.	xx vii.	5	x viij.	xxx iii.	5	xx iij.	xx iiij.
6	viii.	xl ix.	6	x viij.	xl ix.	6	xx iij.	xx vj.
7	ix.	x i.	7	ix.	v.	7	xx iij.	xxviij.
8	ix.	xxxiii.	8	x ix.	x ix.	8	xx iij.	xxx.
9	l ix.	l v.	9	x ix.	xxx iii.	9	xx iij.	xxx ij.
10	x	x vii.	10	x ix.	xl vii.	10	xx iij.	xxx iiij.
11	x	xx ix.	11	xx.	i.	11	xx iij.	xxx iiij.
12	x	i.	12	xx.	l iiii.	12	xx iij.	xxx iiij.
13	x	i. xx iiii.	13	xx.	xx.	13	xx iij.	xxx ij.
14	x	i xl iiii.	14	xx.	xxxviii.	14	xx iij.	xxx i.
15	x	ii. v.	15	xx	l j.	15	xx iij.	xxx.
16	x	ii. xx vi.	16	xx.	l i.	16	xx iij.	xx viii.
17	x	ii. xl vi.	17	xx	i. xx iiij.	17	xx iij.	xx iiij.
18	x	iii. vii.	18	xx	i. xx v.	18	xx iij.	xx iij.
19	x	iii. xx vii.	19	xx	i. xxx vj.	19	xx iij.	x ix.
20	x	iii. xl vii.	20	xx	i. xl vj.	20	xx iij.	v.
21	x	iiii. vii.	21	xx	i. l v.	21	xx iij.	i.
22	x	iiii. xx vii.	22	xx	i. iiii.	22	xx iij.	vj.
23	x	iiii. xl vi.	23	xx	ii. x iij.	23	xx iij.	j.
24	x	v. v.	24	xx	ii. xx j.	24	xx ii.	l vj.
25	x	v. xx iiii.	25	xx	ii. xx ix.	25	xx ii.	l.
26	x	v. xl ii.	26	xx	ii. xl iii.	26	xx ii.	xl iii.
27	x	vi. i.	27	xx	ii. xl iiii.	27	xx ii.	xl iiij.
28	x	vi. x ix.	28	xx	ii. l j.	28	xx ii.	xxviii.
29	x	vi. xxxvii	29	xx	ii. l vj.	29	xx ii.	xx.
30	x	vi. l v.	30	xx	iii. j.	30	xx ii.	x ij.
31	x	vii. l iii.				31	xx ii.	iiii.

The last pieces of the pilot's puzzle

Reckoning latitude at sea was fairly simple, but keeping track of east-west longitude was a bugbear for centuries.

Calculating longitude involves not only accurate celestial sightings but also complex mathematics and exact knowledge of time. The explorers attempted to figure east-west movement by plotting a compass course and estimating the distance made good along it. Speed was taken by observing how long it took a chip of wood tossed off the bow to travel the length of the ship.

But the computations could never be more than just a rough guess. Along with such unknowns as drift and magnetic variation, the early navigators could measure time only by woefully inaccurate instruments like the sundial and sandglass.

A way of telling time at night was by the position of the polestar and its Guard Star Kochab. The nocturlabe, below, shows the polestar centered in a compass rose and radiating lines marking the midnight location of Kochab at various times of the year. The hour was read by how far Kochab had traveled from its midnight position.

When the sundial went to sea, it took on the form of an ivory cylinder with a beaklike indicator that, when pointed into the sun, cast its shadow back onto the shaft at the calibration for the correct hour. Known as the chilindre, or pillar dial, this instrument had to be recalibrated for any major change in latitude to allow for the varying altitude of the sun.

The sandglass was the basic timepiece for ships of the 15th, 16th and 17th centuries. Most often built to measure a half hour or an hour at a time, it was perfectly adequate for marking the four-hour intervals of the watch, but it was much less reliable for figuring the distance covered each day, and was totally useless for calculating longitude. Among other flaws, it tended to clog in humid weather.

voyage and headed out to sea to elude contrary winds and currents close to the coast. Not until he had been sailing for nine or 10 weeks and come more than 30° south of the equator—presumably reckoning that he had reached the lattitude of the Cape of Good Hope—did he come about and head east again. But by this time, as everyone aboard was aware, he had sailed a formidable—and uncertain—distance from land in any direction. Da Gama showed himself to be a supreme navigator. But for all the crewmen knew, he might have been taking them on a mad dash to nowhere. The days turned into weeks, and the months accumulated with few signs of life save an occasional whale or school of porpoise.

At last, on November 1, the explorers sighted some drifting gulf-weed—a sign that land might not be far away. Three days later they found confirmation; the leadsman, sounding the ocean floor, cried out 110 fathoms (about 660 feet) and shelving. At 9 o'clock on the morning of November 4, land rose into miraculous view. The first ship to spot it signaled to the one behind, which in turn conveyed it to the next; and the diarist recorded, with understated relief: "We then drew near to each other, and having put on our gala clothes, we saluted the captain major by firing our bombards, and dressed the ships with flags and standards."

Da Gama and his men had every reason to celebrate in a far wilder fashion. They had been at sea for an unprecedented three months and a day and had come an incredible 4,500 miles since leaving the Cape Verde Islands. What was more, they had done so with only a few facts to go by. When da Gama plunged headlong into the ocean's vast expanse on August 3, all he knew for certain were the latitudes of the Cape Verdes, 16° N., which he was leaving behind, and the Cape of Good Hope, 34° S., for which he was aiming. He had no ocean charts, no tables of winds and currents, no instruments for measuring longitude (pages 93-96) and not a single landmark to help him guess where he was. With little save his own unwavering nerve—a self-possession that clearly gave reassurance to his men—he had, while passing through a feature-less sea, negotiated the full length of a giant continent and then fetched up almost exactly as promised. When he went ashore with his large wooden astrolabe, so he could take a sighting on solid land instead of a bobbing ship, he found that he was only about 1° north of the Cape of Good Hope. The undertaking was among the most audacious in all the annals of the sea; in the execution, it was nothing short of a triumph.

In a sheltered anchorage that he named St. Helena Bay, da Gama careened and overhauled his travel-worn ships. Here the explorers encountered their first humans since leaving the Cape Verde Islands, and the diarist was ready with his journal to note his observations. "The inhabitants of this country are tawny-colored," he wrote, adding, with medieval regard for modesty, that they "wear sheaths over their virile members." They wore very little else, except a few scanty skins and copper beads in their ears. But one thing he found familiar. "Their numerous dogs resemble those of Portugal, and bark like them," he wrote.

The people were the Hottentots, and encountering them, the Portuguese made an error of judgment that might well have cost them the life of their leader before they ever reached the cape. The Hottentots appeared at first to be cordial—the bells and rings the Portuguese had brought along were received with glee, and the people were communicative enough for the Portuguese to find out that they lived on the meat of seal, whale and gazelle and on various plants. But when one of da Gama's officers, Fernão Velloso, ventured inland to visit a village, the Hottentots turned on him and viciously drove him back to the beach, shouting imprecations and hurling their fishing spears. In the ensuing fracas, da Gama—who rushed to Velloso's aid on hearing the shouts of alarm—was wounded in the leg. The Portuguese were astonished, says the journal, "because we looked upon these people as men of little spirit, quite incapable of violence." That was the first of many mistakes that were to put the Portuguese in jeopardy throughout their journey.

Da Gama's wound proved superficial, and the fleet was ready to sail from St. Helena Bay at dawn on November 16. Two days' travel brought them in sight of the Cape of Good Hope, and except for some troublesome winds they rounded it without incident—traveling 132 miles in six days. Continuing east, they reached the area now called Mossel Bay.

At Mossel Bay about 90 Africans came out of the bushes and down to the strand to gape at the ships when they dropped anchor. This time when da Gama went ashore he took the precaution of doing so with an armed party. To his pleasant surprise, he found the natives friendly. Indeed, they serenaded the visitors with gorahs, flutelike instruments, "making a pretty harmony," the diarist noted—and they were eager to barter. For three bracelets da Gama's men bought a black ox from their new acquaintances. "This ox we dined off on Sunday," the diarist recorded, adding with ingenuous chauvinism: "We found him very fat, and his meat as toothsome as the beef in Portugal."

With the cape rounded and welcome, if cautious, human contact reestablished, the first leg of the voyage was over. Da Gama's men had almost reached the point where the Dias expedition had left off; from now on, he and his men would be sailing uncharted waters. He took some time for consolidation and transferred the remaining supplies to the three major vessels. The cumbersome storeship was burned, probably to prevent its falling into alien hands, and the metal fittings were raked from the coals for use in the surviving vessels. Da Gama then moved on.

Up around Africa's tip the travelers went, beating northeast against a northerly wind and a punishing southwesterly current, and enduring a storm that scattered the ships for a day. Regrouping and keeping the coast in sight, they noted the last stone marker left by Dias 10 years before, and noted also that the terrain was becoming wooded with increasingly taller trees. But in their determination to get on with their mission, they did not stop to explore. They observed Christmas Day by bestowing the name Natal (Portuguese for the holiday) on the gently sloping uplands that they passed. The next week, possibly to escape the contrary current, da Gama sailed out to sea again, and soon he had cause to wonder at the wisdom of his move. No land appeared, and the water supply ran so low that daily rations had to be reduced to a meager *quartilho*—three fourths of a pint per man. The meat had to be cooked in brine, and some of the crew—too long without sufficient fresh food and water—began to grow weak with scurvy. Da Gama once again headed in to shore. At the Zavora River the men landed to careen their ships, secure fresh supplies and give the scurvy cases recovery time. The mainmast of Paulo da Gama's *São Rafael* had developed a serious crack, and they repaired it before putting out to sea again. In this zigzag fashion it took them until March to go 1,700 miles up the coast.

But on the second day of that month, a whole new panorama opened up before them. The primitive green woodland gave way to white-washed houses veiled in flowering vines, and gleaming mosques that thrust their slender minarets above the rooftops. Sailing closer, da Gama and his men found a port, its wharves teeming with sharp-sterned dhows and other seagoing vessels with sturdy sails skillfully woven of palm fronds. The expedition had arrived at the city of Mozambique—and the threshold of Moslem civilization.

Mozambique was one of a string of independent city-states that lined the East African coast. Jealously ruled by rival sultans, these principalities had little to do with one another—and even less contact with their country cousins in the bush. The Mozambicans and their neighbors spoke Swahili at home and Arabic in the market place—where they sold their cotton, ivory, timber and gold for Chinese porcelain, Persian rubies, Indian spices and Arabian dates. On the profits of that lively exchange they dressed in fine linen robes and turban-like headgear made of silk embroidered with gold thread.

Here, clearly, was an opportunity to initiate the diplomacy with which his king had charged him, and da Gama plunged ahead. Safely anchored, the Portuguese invited the Sultan aboard the *São Gabriel* for a meal, during which da Gama tried to dispense bounty from his store of presents. Unwittingly, he was committing his second error of the voyage. The tiny bracelets and little bells had served well among the untutored tribesmen in the bush; here they made a sorry showing. The Sultan was unseduced—and impolite. "He treated all we gave him with contempt," the diarist noted ruefully, "and asked for scarlet cloth, of which we had none." For all the thought and money that had gone into building, staffing and lading the ships for this epic voyage, the Portuguese had woefully underestimated their quarry. They were in a land where pearls changed hands by the basketful and trading vessels carried gold and silver. They had not brought anything worth trading for such goods.

The sailors fared not much better with the inhabitants of Mozambique than had da Gama with the Sultan. Their glass beads fetched some goats and pigeons, but that was about all. At length, with an indignant cannonade to show the Mozambicans what he thought, da Gama took leave of the city and headed north, hoping for better luck elsewhere.

He thought he had found it 800 miles north along the coast at Mombasa, the area's most populous city, where some 10,000 citizens lived on an island hard by the mainland. Coming into the steamy, palm-fringed harbor and seeing the dhows and other vessels all decked in flags, da Gama construed the scene as one of welcome and got out all his bunting to respond in kind. But the Mombasans were celebrating the end of fasting during the Moslem month of Ramadan, not the arrival of da Gama. After repulsing a couple of packs of yelling, evil-looking thugs who swarmed out in boats and tried to board his ships, da Gama put out to sea again.

The explorers' prospects brightened immeasurably at the next stop along the coast; this was Malindi, a smaller city than their first two ports of call, but one prepared to offer good water and plentiful food supplies—and, most importantly, a friendly welcome. In the roadstead, they came upon four odd-looking ships; unlike the Arab vessels they had seen so far, these carried guns that returned the Portuguese salutes. Da Gama and his men struck up a conversation with the crews—curious-looking fellows with brownish skin and long beards and hair. To their intense joy, the explorers learned that the vessels hailed from India, the very destination da Gama so avidly sought. The exotic strangers were invited aboard Paulo da Gama's *São Rafael,* where they were shown an altarpiece embellished with a figure of the Virgin Mary at the foot of the cross. The strangers prostrated themselves before the icon and returned with offerings of cloves and pepper—a performance that the Portuguese, so eager to find congenial companions in this alien world, took as a sign of religious faith. They rejoiced to think that at long last they had come upon some of the "Indian Christians" they had been led to expect. Actually, they had met their first Hindus, who were kneeling before the Virgin in the mistaken belief that she was one of their own idols.

The Portuguese had other, more practical reasons for rejoicing. The local sultan, a vision in damask and green satin, seated on a bronze chair and sheltered from the tropical sun by a crimson parasol, sailed to the middle of the harbor to meet the captain major. Da Gama made his acquaintance cautiously, greeting his visitor with a recital by the ship's trumpeters, but keeping a retinue of men-at-arms at hand. He need not have worried. The Sultan was most obliging. In fact, he was a bitter rival of the Sultan they had just left in Mombasa, and he saw in da Gama a possible ally. Far from taking umbrage at the modest offerings that da Gama pulled from his store of favors, the Sultan responded with lavish gifts of cloves, pepper and six sheep, and offered his services.

What the Portuguese needed most now was a pilot to lead them on the next and crucial step of their journey. Having reached the last East African port of any size, they were ready to venture across the Indian Ocean. The Sultan provided a navigator who was both expert and trustworthy. It was well that he did, for the route was hazardous in the extreme. The direct-line distance was 2,300 miles northeast. But the way was blocked by a maze of islands and atolls, through which a course had to be threaded. Many of the atolls projected too little above the water's surface to be spotted from a distance and plunged too steeply below it to be detected in advance by sounding; for the unwary and inexperienced, there was constant danger of running aground on a hull-gutting coral atoll.

The Malindi pilot seemed to know every knob and finger of reef, and with his skill—plus a timely assist from a southwest monsoon that was just beginning to stir—da Gama's fleet made the trip not only in safety but in a speedy 27 days, averaging nearly 100 miles a day.

On May 18, 1497, they made landfall on the Malabar Coast, about 50 miles north of the port of Calicut. For the crew the most memorable feature of the trip was the reappearance, on the sixth day out, of the North Star—proof they had recrossed the equator and returned to the Northern Hemisphere. For the nation whose flag they flew, the voyage would mean excitement on a grander scale. After 60 years of questing, the sea voyage to India had been made. The diarist recorded the moment with simple understatement: their Malindi pilot told them this was "Calicut, and that this was the country we desired to go to."

The explorers' first glimpse of Asia showed them a verdant land of sparkling beaches and tall palms, and in the distance under gathering thunderclouds the ramparts of a mountain range. And they were pleased to find an even more lavish welcome than at Malindi. First, an emissary from the Zamorin, or king, of Calicut came on board to invite them to the palace. Then, when da Gama went ashore with 13 of his officers, an escort of 200 men with unsheathed swords led them, with trumpets blaring and muskets firing, on a gala parade through the city's wide, palm-shaded streets. From the heady perspective of a palanquin borne by six Indians, da Gama had a king's eye view of the multitude that crowded the streets, the doorways and rooftops to watch.

En route to the palace the procession came to an imposing edifice hewn of stone and faced with tiles; at its entrance was a bronze pillar that to the diarist looked "as tall as a mast." Here the paraders paused: "In this church the captain major said his prayers, and we with him," the diarist recorded. What the Portuguese had mistaken for a Christian church was, of course, a temple to the Hindu gods (*pages 108-109*). At the palace, they were ushered into an antechamber, and there was the Zamorin—a marvel of elaborate indolence as he reclined on a green velvet couch, holding a gold spittoon and chewing nuts. He called for fruit; in came bananas and melons, and he bade his guests refresh themselves.

After a few days in Calicut, da Gama judged that the diplomatic moment had come to proffer his familiar gift of caps and beads. But when he informed the Zamorin's agents of his intention, they stopped him. "When they saw the present they laughed at it," noted the diarist, "saying that it was not a thing to offer a king, that the poorest merchant from Mecca or any other part of India gave more, and that if he wanted to make a present it should be in gold." From that moment on, relations with the Zamorin deteriorated rapidly. At one point the Zamorin's men arrested and briefly imprisoned several of the Portuguese in an altercation over the payment of harbor tolls. The men were released when da Gama took some Hindus hostage. Any real trade was obviously impossible.

The Calicut merchants regarded the Portuguese with undisguised contempt. They not only refused to trade but spat on the ground and uttered insults. It was not just the inferior quality of the Portuguese goods that set them off; that simply fueled a natural antagonism that would have been present had da Gama arrived bearing coffers of pure gold. It turned out that the merchants in this Hindu land were almost all Moslems. They hated Christians and had no intention of sharing their lucrative trade in spices and other treasures. Appeals to the Zamorin were dismissed; much of the kingdom's revenues came from these merchants and, not surprisingly, they had considerable influence at court.

Balked at every turn but determined not to go home empty-handed, da Gama took to sending the men from his ships in twos and threes to swap what they could with waterfront hangers-on. Even there they met noth-

With the hands-aloft gesture required by local custom, Vasco da Gama, in his first diplomatic encounter with an Asian court, salutes the Zamorin of Calicut, a minor potentate of the Malabar Coast. To show humility, the palace guards cover their mouths while in the presence of the Zamorin. Da Gama's chronicler reported that the official consumed great quantities of mildly narcotic betel nuts, a platter of which is being brought in to him by the servant at right.

ing but disappointment. The best they could do was to sell their trifles at a tenth of their Portuguese value; a shirt that fetched 300 reis in Lisbon brought the Indian equivalent of only 30. They managed to accumulate some cloves and cinnamon and a handful of precious stones—but the sum total made a miserably poor showing for a mission that had set out with such lofty aspirations for diplomacy and trade.

After three months, da Gama had had enough. On August 29 he and his men sailed from Calicut. They headed north along the coast and did some minor reconnoitering. Finding nothing of interest but a few small sheltered islands somewhere south of Goa, they careened and caulked their ships for the voyage home. In mid-October they entered the Indian Ocean on a southwest course for Africa, whence they had come.

The return voyage was a difficult one, plagued by evil fortune from the start. The Portuguese no longer had their Malindi pilot—he had unaccountably vanished during their unhappy stay in Calicut—and they had to thread their own path through the treacherous, atoll-dotted waters. They had chosen the wrong time of year and had to fight alternating calms and head winds. To cover the same distance that had taken only 27 days coming over took three excruciating months going back.

To make matters infinitely worse, they had insufficient food for such a long voyage. Now the men discovered the full horrors of scurvy, of which they had had only an inkling the previous spring. Their gums turned livid, puffy and rotten, then oozed black blood and crept over their teeth. Their legs turned weak and gangrenous. The worst afflicted had too little strength even to fight off the ships' rats that gnawed at the soles of their feet. As one after another sank into a coma and died, the survivors feebly pushed the corpses over the side—themselves so listless that any exertion seemed to require a Herculean effort. "Thirty of our men died in this manner," wrote the chronicler, adding: "I assure you that if this state of affairs had continued for another fortnight, there would have been no men at all to navigate the ships." Vasco da Gama, presumably having a constitution as strong as his will, seems to have been one of the few to escape the disease, and his brother Paulo, as compassionate as Vasco was forbidding, moved about among the sick dispensing unguents and potions from his personal stores.

Somehow all three ships made it to Malindi—and there they found blessed relief. The Sultan, previously so helpful, now saved their lives by sending out to the stricken explorers a little fleet of bumboats laden with meat, fowl and eggs—and oranges, which relieved the scurvy. He also granted da Gama's request for an elephant tusk for the King of Portugal, and for permission to leave a *padrão* on Malindi soil. That stone marker—almost the last of its kind to commemorate Portuguese exploration—was to stand near the palace, a testament not only to the hardy mariners who had found the way there but also to the courtesies of the Sultan of Malindi. Without his help, they might well have been halted on the threshold of India—or on the first lap of the journey home.

Even with the dramatic recovery of many of his men from scurvy, da Gama found on leaving Malindi that he still had too few sailors left to crew three ships. So he sadly beached and burned Paulo's *São Rafael*—first saving the statue that represented her guardian angel—and redis-

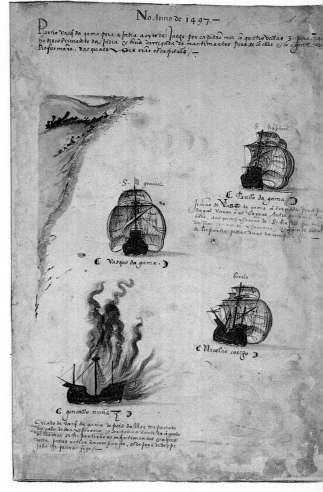

A page from a 16th Century catalogue of Portuguese ships shows da Gama's fleet (clockwise from upper left): the São Gabriel, the fleet's flagship; the São Rafael, captained by da Gama's brother Paulo and, like the São Gabriel, designed specially for the voyage by Bartolomeu Dias; the Berrio, the light, swift caravel of Nicolau Coelho (shown here incorrectly as a square-rigged carrack); and the storeship, which was emptied and put to the torch shortly after the fleet sailed around the Cape of Good Hope.

tributed the remaining crew between the *São Gabriel* and the *Berrio*.

Relentlessly now, they pushed south along the East African coast, avoiding hostile Mombasa and Mozambique, catching penguins and anchovies where they could for food. They redoubled the Cape of Good Hope in March of 1499 and had the satisfaction of heading north again and nearing familiar waters once more. "We pursued our route with a great desire of reaching home," the diarist noted. Those were almost his last recorded words. Whether he succumbed to disease or to the sea or whether the urge to record diminished with the quickening drive to get home is not explained by later chroniclers. But the diary ends abruptly on the 25th of April, somewhere off the coast of Guinea.

One who is known to have succumbed to sickness in the final days of the two-year epic was the gentle Paulo da Gama. The illness itself was not recorded by later chroniclers who wrote secondhand accounts of the voyage. It was only stated that he had been ailing since rounding the cape and that by the time the fleet reached the Cape Verde Islands he was beyond help. In a desperate effort to ease his brother's final moments, Vasco da Gama detoured to the Azores to take the dying man ashore. There Paulo died and was buried in the Franciscan monastery.

Da Gama arrived back in Lisbon sometime in late August or early September to a tumultuous welcome from his king and countrymen. He had been gone just over two years, had traveled a stupendous 27,000 miles—enough to circle the globe, had he known it. He had returned with only 54 of his original 170 adventurers. It was a high price in human terms, but no one gave that a thought, least of all King Manuel I. The King spared no effort in exploiting the national euphoria at home and advertising the triumph abroad. He had da Gama elaborately paraded through the city on September 18. He struck a handsome 10-crusado commemorative gold coin. He issued pamphlets to be distributed by the dozens all over European capitals. At Belem, a little village near where the Tagus meets the ocean, he built a great church overlooking the site that the Portuguese were forever to hold sacred as "the shore of tears for those that go, and the shore of pleasure for those that return."

And triumphantly, Manuel wrote his Castilian rivals, the monarchs Ferdinand and Isabella of Spain. "Most high and excellent Prince and Princess, most potent Lord and Lady!" he saluted them with royal bravado, and then went on about the "large cities, large edifices and rivers, and great populations" that his invincible explorers had found—not forgetting the spices, precious stones and "mines of gold." No mention of scurvy and hunger; no hint that more than 100 men had died; no suggestion that hostile Moslem rulers and merchants had impeded almost every step of the way; no intimation that the handful of spices and gems that da Gama had brought back represented but a token of trade.

In marked contrast to the secrecy with which his royal predecessors had cloaked past voyages, Manuel was only too eager to crow about this one. He was putting all Europe on notice that his nation had reached India and meant to claim the route. He wrote in terms dazzling enough to command attention but vague enough to preserve a sense of mystery.

In tallying the net gains of the expedition, Portugal had reason to boast, for the voyage had been a triumph of national teamwork and

A wooden statue of the Archangel Rafael is all that remains of Paulo da Gama's ship, the São Rafael, which was burned on the return voyage from India after scurvy had killed most of the crew. Vasco, in memory of Paulo, who died a few months later, kept the statue for the rest of his life.

personal endurance. What da Gama and his surviving companions had done, others could do again—and there were compelling reasons to continue. By 1499, when da Gama returned, the price of pepper in Venice—where Portugal and every other nation in Europe had to buy it—had almost doubled since 1495. If da Gama brought back only a handful of spices, he brought back with it the revelation that the hundredweight of pepper sold for 80 ducats in Venice could be had in Calicut for the equivalent of three ducats. At such a markup—and with comparable markups for cinnamon, cloves, nutmeg, silk, gold and gems—clearly the voyage to India was worthwhile, despite its monumental cost. The Venetians, preoccupied with fighting off the Turks, who were thrusting their empire westward, scarcely noticed the Portuguese feat. The remaining obstacle was the hostility of the Moslems, who had prior claims to the spices, gems and gold that Portugal now coveted. In the eyes of the Portuguese monarchy, the problem became one of eliminating the Moslem grip on trade. Portugal next set out to do just that.

Less than six months after da Gama's triumphal progress through Lisbon, Portugal was ready with another expedition—this one a massive armada of 13 ships transporting 1,200 men, including trained soldiers. They sailed under Pedro Alvares Cabral, a 32-year-old nobleman with no recorded sailing experience but with family connections at court; his father had served as a counselor to João II, and Pedro and two of his brothers now served Manuel in the same role.

Profiting by da Gama's wide swing out into the Atlantic, but not following precisely the same path, Cabral took his fleet so far west into the Atlantic Ocean that in about six weeks he sighted Brazil. Whether the sighting was accidental or whether it was a preplanned excursion in search of land already thought to be there is an open question; Cabral's voyage was clearly mounted for the purpose of inaugurating trade with the Orient. But Spain, Portugal's rival, was by this time planting an imperial foot on other points in the Western Hemisphere, and under the terms of the Treaty of Tordesillas (page 91) the new-found land was Portugal's for the taking. Whether instructed to do so or not, Cabral killed two birds with one stone on this voyage, claiming Brazil for his country and making his voyage to the Far East. Brazil would be colonized—but that would be much later in the century. Cabral's most pressing concern now was to turn east and get on with his main business.

The fleet was scarcely under way again when a comet appeared in the Southern sky and hung there for eight nights, pointing toward the Cape of Good Hope and seeming to 15th Century sailors to bode some cataclysmic event. As if to confirm the superstition, the comet had no sooner disappeared when the wind died strangely away—only to return in hurricane force, scattering all the ships and sinking four. Despite the excursion to Brazil and the hurricane, Cabral got all the way to Calicut in just six months. And now began an epoch of signal ruthlessness.

The Zamorin was reluctant to receive Cabral. He remembered all too clearly da Gama's paltry offerings, and the Moslem merchants' reactions. But Cabral had come better prepared than da Gama, and set about cajoling the Zamorin. He showered his quarry with lavish presents, among them a silver basin with gilded figures in relief, two silver maces,

The fate of the disaster-prone expedition to India of Pedro Alvares Cabral in 1500 is depicted in pages from a 16th Century record book. Four ships (third row, above, and at right) including one captained by Bartolomeu Dias, were lost with all hands during a South Atlantic tempest; one ran aground and was burned (bottom) and another ship (second row, left) strayed from the fleet and presumably sank. The remaining seven returned to Lisbon with a fortune in spices and stunning news of the discoveries of Brazil and Madagascar.

VARES·CABRAL·ANO·DE·ʃOO·

Nienlao coelho
Jae·fiz
Pedralueſ cabral·
Symao Demjvao So—
Diogus de figueiro
Bortolameu Diaz

two brocaded cushions, two tapestries and a large carpet. Meanwhile, he intimated he would take his trade elsewhere, and slyly threatened harsh punishment if the Zamorin did not see matters his way.

One day when a rival city's ship with a cargo of half a dozen elephants came into port, Cabral sent one of his small caravels against it. The Zamorin "marveled greatly," wrote an anonymous member of Cabral's officers, "that so small a caravel and with so few people could take so large a ship in which were 300 men at arms." Cabral made the Zamorin a present of his prize; and the writer added that the Zamorin "received the ship and the elephants with great pleasure and solace."

After two and a half months of such tactics, the Zamorin was persuaded to sign a treaty designed to give the Portuguese their first foothold in Oriental trading. The treaty was recorded twice: once on a sheet of silver with the Zamorin's signature engraved in gold, which was to be taken back to the King of Portugal, and again on humbler copper with the signature in brass, which was to remain in Calicut. The treaty provided for setting up a depot for collecting spices. Here Cabral installed 70 men to begin assembling a spice cargo to take home to Portugal.

Trouble arose at once. The Moslems smoldered with resentment, and the anonymous officer wrote that they importuned the Zamorin, "telling how we had on land more riches than we had carried to his kingdom, and that we were the worst robbers and thieves in the world." The Portuguese managed to load only two ships; then the Moslems rioted in the streets, and 3,000 stormed the depot, killing 50 of its members. The remaining 20 were severely wounded and reached safety only by swimming out to their ships under a hail of arrows flung from crossbows.

Cabral retaliated by capturing 10 Moslem ships, slaying their officers and crews of 500 or 600 men, seizing their cargoes, and burning the vessels. And because it seemed to him that the Zamorin had treacherously condoned the attack on the depot, he bombarded Calicut, sending the wooden houses of the palm-fringed city up in flames. He then decided to give up on Calicut, and move south to the next port, Cochin.

Here, partly because news of the Portuguese performance at Calicut preceded him, partly because the local ruler was a bitter rival of the Zamorin of Calicut, Cabral had no trouble at all getting down to business. In two weeks he had concluded a new agreement, loaded his ships and installed a new depot to take the place of the one lost at Calicut. It was to be a combination trading post, storehouse and garrison. It would mean that, when later Portuguese ships arrived, they would lose no time in trading; the trading would be done in their absence by Portuguese factors left behind. Newly arriving Portuguese ships would find quantities of spices already purchased, and ready for loading at once.

Cabral had laid the first building block of the Portuguese empire in India. He had also set a pattern. The trade that would fuel that empire would be won by ruthless and costly warring with the Moslem merchants, whose commercial supremacy along the Indian coast had existed for generations, and by playing the Hindu leaders one against another, cajoling here, intimidating there.

When Cabral reached Portugal in the summer of 1501, only seven of his 13 ships and not even half of his 1,200 men had survived. Nonetheless, he had a cargo of salable spices. Reports of its size varied, but according to one rumor that reached Venice, it amounted to 300,000 pounds.

The profits soon poured in. Before the year was out, the Portuguese set up an exchange in Antwerp, and from this central location they began to sell spices to all of Europe—and with their burgeoning wealth to buy copper and silver from the ore-rich principalities of Central Europe. German and Italian bankers flocked to Lisbon, offering liberal credit.

Manuel had another expedition ready the year Cabral returned, and another the next year. With annual voyages, the growth of Portuguese commerce in Europe was so rapid that the little nation soon needed more depots to hold all the spices it could buy in India; setting up more depots meant more men and arms to guard them. Before long, Manuel created a new post to "regulate commerce" in the Indian Ocean and gave its occupant the imposing title of Viceory of India. As first viceroy, he chose Francisco de Almeida, a nobleman who more than a decade earlier had distinguished himself by fighting against the Moors. Setting out in 1505 at the head of a cannon-laden fleet, Almeida interpreted his instructions liberally, not even waiting to reach India before getting on with the job. On the way, he sacked and destroyed Mombasa and captured two other East African ports, Sofala and Kilwa.

Among the officers that Almeida left at the garrison he installed at Kilwa was a young nobleman who was later to become a giant among explorers. His name was Ferdinand Magellan, and he would go down in history as a servant not of Portugal but of her great rival, Spain.

From Kilwa, Almeida took his powerful fleet across the Arabian Sea to the Malabar Coast, where he set about his main mission with great energy—and no little relish. Fortifying a series of harbors, he used them as bases from which to raid Moslem commerce, seizing, looting and burning ships and terrorizing his victims. One Portuguese chronicler, describing the blood reign, reported that Almeida "blew his prisoners from guns before Cananour, saluting the town with their fragments." In four years, Almeida drove Arab shipping from the Malabar Coast.

In 1509 Manuel replaced Almeida, whose three-year term as viceroy had ended, with Affonso de Albuquerque, a 56-year-old graybeard with royal blood in his veins—he was descended from Castilian and Portuguese kings—and a teeming fountain of farsighted schemes in his head. Improving upon Almeida's advances, he carried Portuguese authority inland, acquiring several ingeniously placed and far-flung bases: in 1510 he seized the town of Goa—a shipbuilding port that lay at the northern end of the Malabar Coast—from the Moslems and made it his capital. No mere garrison with transient merchants and fly-by-night sailors and soldiers who came and went by acquiescence of local rulers, Goa was soon a thriving community of 450 settlers. The Portuguese built a loading dock, a monastery, a hospital and so many houses that by 1524 one community leader reported in a letter to the King, "within the circuit of the city there is no unoccupied ground." In 10 short years Portugal had made the leap in India from trading post to full-fledged colony.

Even before then, Albuquerque was reaching farther afield. In 1511 he took Malacca—a vital spice emporium 2,500 miles distant, at the gateway to the China Sea. Four years after that he seized Hormuz, on the

Francisco de Almeida, Portuguese India's first viceroy, cleared the neighboring seas of Moslem and Egyptian ships. Though Portugal held few trading ports, Almeida decreed, "Avoid the annexation of territory; we can spare no men from the navy."

Affonso de Albuquerque, Almeida's successor, rectified Portugal's dearth of territory by taking Goa (right), Malacca and Hormuz. A grandiose scheme to steal Mohammed's corpse to ransom the Holy Land died with Albuquerque in 1515.

doorstep of the Persian Gulf. With those bases, and the colonial capital lying about halfway between them, Portugal now had control over every entrance to the Indian Ocean save one—the Red Sea. And that lone entrance was a small matter. Arab naval power was no match for Portugal's, and the Moslem commercial system as da Gama had found it in 1498 had been wiped out of the Indian Ocean.

Da Gama himself, through most of these years, was living in honored rest at home in Portugal, just off the cathedral square in Evora, in a house decorated with murals of Indian plants and animals. With the titles of Admiral of India and Count of Vidigueira, Dom Vasco, as he was now styled, had three royal pensions amounting to 2,750 crusadoes—an income exceeded by only half a dozen noblemen and eight bishops in all the land—plus a lucrative share of the anchorage dues paid by the trading vessels at Malacca, Goa and Hormuz. When he died on Christmas Eve in 1524 at the age of 64, he had lived long enough to know that, though rival Spain had discovered a New World in the West, Portugal had found the way to the East—and the lion's share of European maritime commerce. His sovereign, Manuel I, had adopted the grandiose title of "King, by the Grace of God, of Portugal and of the Algarves, both on this side of the sea and beyond it in Africa, Lord of Guinea and of the Conquest, Navigation, and Commerce of Ethiopia, Arabia, Persia and India"—a title that envious rivals reduced to "the Grocer King."

A plethora of churches and crosses marks the town of Goa as a Portuguese stronghold on India's west coast. The heart of the colony is well protected by a red brick wall with gates and battlements, while a sturdy fort guards the sea approach. Between the fort and the wall and along the northern coastline are Goa's vegetable gardens and fruit orchards.

Marvels of India Oriental through Western eyes

Upon his return to Portugal from the Malabar Coast of India in 1499, Vasco da Gama was convinced that he had discovered a remote and exotic but nonetheless Christian culture. Though dark skinned, the friendly people he encountered appeared European in their features. More important, they seemed to him to recognize Christian deities; indeed, one idol they worshipped bore a close resemblance to the Virgin Mary. But as later Portuguese—traders and colonists lured by the sea route da Gama opened—sailed to what they termed "India Oriental," it became clear that the Indians were a very different people with very different beliefs. Some of the wonderment the Indians evoked in the Portuguese is captured in these watercolors by an unknown Portuguese artist traveling through India in the mid-1500s.

In actuality the Indians of the Malabar Coast were subjects of the empire of Vijayanagar—the last stronghold of Hindu faith in a land increasingly ruled by Moslem invaders from the northwest. This Hindu enclave stretched from Cape Comorin at the southern tip of the subcontinent 500 miles up into the peninsula. Its capital city, Vijayanagar, was ringed with three walls, and from here the emperors of the 160-year-old Vijayanagar Dynasty held sway over a rigid social system encompassing five orders from lowly untouchables to privileged Brahmans. Administrative control was exercised through local lords, or rajahs, who also mustered the hordes of infantry, cavalry and war elephants that safeguarded the empire from the Moslem interlopers lusting after the immense Hindu wealth. A chronicler marveled: "The jewelers sell publicly in the bazaars pearls, rubies, emeralds and diamonds."

The Portuguese had a more difficult time comprehending the Hindu religion, which bore only a superficial resemblance to Christianity. At the heart of it was the doctrine of reincarnation, which held that every soul was struggling through a series of rebirths toward a perfect state vaguely identified as a union with God. The deity da Gama mistook for the Virgin was probably Devaki, mother of Krishna, who is among the most celebrated of a baffling pantheon of Hindu gods. One scornful Portuguese finally concluded that the Hindus "have many foolish tales about their idols, such as it is out of reason for men to believe."

Set apart from humans by their extra arms, the chief gods of the Hindu pantheon stand prepared to exercise their all-reaching powers. According to Hindu texts, Brahma (right) created the world, Vishnu (left) preserves it, and Shiva (center) waits to destroy it; the Portuguese artist mistakenly reversed the labels on the first two figures.

hispar

visno

brama

estes sam deoses:
dos Jintios aqueeles
chamão paguodes:

Attended by servants, the wife of a well-to-do Portuguese colonist curls up comfortably on an Indian version of the sedan chair as she is carried in high style through the countryside. The Portuguese reveled in this mode of transportation, for it elevated them to the status of the uppermost castes. As one settler wrote home, "People are not allowed to make use of litters unless they are cavaliers of the highest rank."

97+ Jente onrada portuguesa da india

112

Gracefully balancing water jars on their heads or filling the vessels at a hillside spring, Indian women in colorful saris go about one of their numerous daily chores. Even though husbands displayed wealth by weighting their wives with bangles, women had been condemned to a life of servitude centuries before by the Hindu lawgiver Manu, who decreed, "A woman is never fit for independence."

baneanas molheres de mer
cadores m̃ Ricos do Reino
de canbaya
· Jintios ·

114

Set to a brisk trot by four herdsmen, a caravan of seven bullocks clip-clops down a road in India. The artist has given the animals expressions of remarkable good humor, and well he might, for the Portuguese noted that the people did not eat oxen or cows. "They hold these animals blessed and when they meet an ox on the highway, they touch him and afterward kiss their hand as a sign of great humility."

62

almocreues canaris. Jintios. quetra
zen triguo dobalaguate aguoa avender.

116

Bearing a turret brimful of warriors and bristling with spears, a war elephant approaches four natives who point out the lumbering terror from a safe position in the hills. Such European-style turrets were figments of the artist's imagination, but the elephants were fearsome enough. As one Portuguese observed, "the elephant is so redoubtable that none awaits his attack if flight is possible."

elefante de guera.

The soldier who completed Columbus' quest

n August 1509 a powerful Portuguese fleet of five heavily armed vessels carrying more than 200 seamen and soldiers sailed east from India to the farthest reaches of the Indian Ocean and beyond—to Malacca, a port in present-day Malaysia that commanded the approaches to Borneo and on to the Moluccas, in the heart of the Spice Islands. Christopher Columbus, flying the flag of Spain, had already made four voyages across the Atlantic to the New World, and a westward passage to the Orient might be discovered at any moment. It was therefore imperative that Portugal remain in the forefront, secure the gains of the eastward passage around Africa, consolidate her control of the Indian Ocean and push on to the Spice Islands, the ultimate objective of all explorers.

Commanding this expedition was Diogo Lopes de Sequeira, a noble who had been a member of the Portuguese king's circle. Among his supporting officers was another nobleman, Ferdinand Magellan. Magellan, who had been sent to Portugal's budding Eastern empire as a king's soldier, would prove himself to be a man of great courage and loyalty.

Sequeira anchored his fleet in Malacca's harbor on September 11, 1509. The harbor was a sight to bedazzle European eyes; there were scores of vessels—Arab, Chinese, Malay and Burmese—loading spices from the crowded quays; the air was heavy with the fragrance of cloves, pepper, cinnamon, ginger and nutmeg. The arrival of the strangers produced a momentary panic, for the harsh deeds of the Europeans in India were not unknown among the Malays. But the ruling sultan was quick to calm his people—and to lay ingenious plans to seize Sequeira's fleet, thus inflicting such a crushing blow upon the Portuguese as would check their move beyond India and into the Far East. Even as he made friendly overtures to Sequeira, the Sultan was secretly bringing forward troops and war elephants from the jungles of the interior and cleverly hiding a fleet of war sampans in a cove.

Gulled by promises of all the pepper and other spices his ships would hold, Sequeira allowed his men to go ashore "as if," in the words of a chronicler, "they had been at anchor off the city of Lisbon." Before long, close to 100 men and all but one of the ships' boats had left for shore. While the Portuguese rowed blithely up to the quays, a large number of Malay craft congregated around the Portuguese vessels, and a number of Malays climbed aboard, ostensibly to trade.

In all the fleet the only men to sense a trap were Magellan and Garcia de Sousa, captain of one of the ships. Sousa cleared his decks of Malays and sent Magellan in the sole remaining ship's boat to warn Sequeira. Magellan found Sequeira on his flagship, playing chess with a Malay chief while half a dozen armed Malays watched. With great calm, Magellan warned Sequeira of the impending danger. Just then screams of "Treachery! treachery!" were heard from shore. Sequeira leaped to his feet before the Malays around him could strike, upset the chessboard and ran on deck, ordering his men to drive the enemy from the ship. Portuguese seamen opened fire with muskets and poured a murderous broadside of cannon shot into the Malay craft crowding alongside.

Dashing through the battle, Magellan leaped back into his boat and ordered his oarsmen to row full speed for land in a desperate attempt to

A clear, direct gaze and forceful prominent features mark this portrait of Ferdinand Magellan, painted some years after his death by an unknown 16th Century artist. In tribute to his epic passage around South America, the Latin legend reads: "Most Renowned for Having Conquered the Narrows of the Antarctic"—which was known ever after as the Strait of Magellan.

save his comrades onshore from slaughter. Heedless of his own safety, he fought his way to the pier to rescue 40 Portuguese who had escaped the butchery of the initial surprise attack. Beating off a swarm of Malays who tried to board his boat, Magellan somehow got the surviving seamen on board and, braving lances and arrows, rowed them safely back.

In the aftermath, Sequeira anchored in the roadstead and waited a day or two in the hope that he might ransom the survivors among his 60 missing men. But the Sultan refused to negotiate, and in the end, Sequeira sent ashore the corpses of two Malay captives with arrows through their brains and a message attached to their battered bodies—"thus the King of Portugal avenged the treason of his enemies." The Portuguese fleet then raised sail for India.

Ferdinand Magellan's quick-witted and courageous actions at the Battle of Malacca were a sure measure of the man. Bold and tough, possessed of an inflexible will, ambitious for wealth and personal glory, this young noble might have won renown as a general were he not destined for the sea and greatness as an explorer. At that, Magellan was never a master mariner in the sense of being a nonpareil ship handler or a supremely expert navigator—though he gained enough of both skills to see him through. His great strengths were his soldierly qualities, his force of mind, his spirit of self-sacrifice and his ability to motivate and lead men. The pity for Portugal was that fateful circumstance would turn him from his native land to neighboring Spain, where he would find support for what had become his life's mission: to succeed where Columbus had failed, and find a passage west across the vast ocean to the Spice Islands of the East. With only the barest of resources, Magellan would embark across the Atlantic and search southward down the interminable, unknown coast of South America; he would endure vicissitudes of the worst sort before at last he and his men would stumble across a strait leading from the Atlantic to the Pacific. And then the explorers would set off on an even more hazardous journey across that immense and fearsome ocean on a course for the treasure-laden Moluccas.

Some historians have suggested, with poetic license, that Magellan's granite will was bred into him by the stark mountainous country of northern Portugal where he was born about 1480—there is no record of the exact date. His family were proud but impecunious members of the minor nobility; the stony, unyielding land produced little to make a man rich. To give young Ferdinand a better chance in life, his father sent him off to Lisbon at about age 12 to become a page to Queen Leonor, wife of King João II. Like so many young Portuguese nobles of his day, he was to complete his education at the court—after which he hoped to receive a royal appointment as a military commander or as a colonial administrator. But there was another possibility.

All through his youth, Magellan was stirred by tales of the great Portuguese explorers—of Dias conquering the oceans around Africa, of da Gama reaching India and returning with intoxicating news of the fabulous spices, ivory, jewels and gold in the East. Magellan began his own career by shipping out as a soldier-adventurer on the 1505 expedition to India commanded by Francisco de Almeida. For seven years he served in

Amerigo Vespucci, who explored 6,000 miles of South American coastline on a 1502 voyage to the New World that would bear his name, was better known as a nautical scientist. He is shown here charting stellar activity with what seems to be a sphere but is identified by the artist as an astrolabe. Additional navigational equipment is on the table.

the budding colonies, suffering several wounds and proving himself a brave and resourceful officer—as during the rescue of Sequeira at Malacca. And when in 1512 he finally sailed for home from Cochin, India, there occurred another incident that told something of importance about Magellan's character—namely, his powerful sense of honor.

Scarcely had his ship and a companion vessel cleared Cochin harbor when they ran aground on a shoal. The crews were able to off-load some provisions and cargo into the ships' boats and row to a nearby island.

Here a furious debate took place. The captains of the two vessels announced that they and their officers would take the ships' boats and row back to the Indian mainland for help. Quite naturally, the seamen did not much take to the idea of being marooned on a barren rock and were about to rush the boats when Magellan intervened. He calmly stated that he would stay behind with the crews as a hostage to ensure the other officers' good faith. Magellan's cool and selfless action defused the explosive situation. The officers reached India in eight days and fulfilled their vow to send help, dispatching a caravel that rescued all the men unharmed. The ordinary seamen remained devoted to Magellan, as in later years other seamen would cleave to the side of this extraordinary man and follow him into the void.

How Magellan reached Portugal after the shipwreck is unknown, but by June 12, 1512, he was in Lisbon and again a member of the King's household. Within a year, however, he was called upon to fight once more when war broke out between the Portuguese and the Moors. Again he was wounded, this time severely. In a battle in Morocco he suffered a lance thrust in one leg; the blade evidently damaged a tendon behind his knee. For the rest of his life, Magellan walked with such a pronounced limp that one historian mistakenly wrote that he had a club foot.

As a sinecure, the lame Magellan was put in charge of the vast booty the Portuguese had captured from the Moors. But now commenced his downfall and eventual self-exile from the land of his birth. Some of the booty—a quantity of livestock—inexplicably disappeared. Magellan was held accountable. Worse, he was accused of selling the animals back to the Moors and pocketing the proceeds.

In a fury of rage and injured pride, Magellan sailed from Morocco to Lisbon to see King Manuel I in person and to clear his name. However, a letter reached the monarch before Magellan did, not only repeating the charges but adding that Magellan was absent without leave. The King coldly refused to grant Magellan a private audience and ordered him back to Africa. Magellan obediently returned to Morocco, where he stood trial for theft and was cleared of all charges. But the damage was done. Manuel, a suspicious and vengeful man, never again trusted Magellan. When the battered veteran once more presented himself at court and petitioned for a small allowance in recognition of his long service, Manuel turned him down with anger and contempt and even suggested that Magellan could, for all the King cared, sell his services elsewhere.

Rejected, frustrated, aching from old wounds and as poor as ever—what wealth he had managed to accumulate in the East had been lost in the shipwreck—Magellan began to brood about a scheme that, if it worked, would bring him both monetary reward and a glorious place in history. Like Columbus years before, he envisioned an easier route to the Indies by sailing west instead of east.

Magellan began by studying all the charts, maps and pilots' logs that he could find in Lisbon's Casa das Indias e da Guiné, the House of the Indies and the Guinea Coast, where the nation's maritime archives were kept. He also associated with an eccentric scholar named Ruy Faleiro, an unsuccessful applicant for the post of royal astronomer in Portugal.

From these sources, Magellan filled in his knowledge of the voyages of discovery that had been sent westward across the Atlantic. He learned that Columbus had scouted much of the Central American coast without finding either the Indies or a break in the land leading westward. Magellan learned as well that in 1497 the Genoese Giovanni Caboto, sailing under the orders of England's King Henry VII (to whom he was known as John Cabot), had found what seemed a very big and solid continent to the north of Columbus' explorations. Reading on, Magellan studied the logs of Pedro Alvares Cabral, who, following da Gama out to India, had been blown clear across the Atlantic and had bumped into Brazil. He also read with fascination the account of the Florentine navigator, Amerigo Vespucci, who in 1501 had struck Brazil in the area of today's Natal and journeyed down the South American coast, possibly reaching the Río de la Plata or even Patagonia. And Magellan knew as well that in 1513 Vasco Núñez de Balboa, a Spanish colonist in Panama, had crossed the narrow Isthmus of Panama and had seen before him a body of salt water that he believed to be a new ocean, distinct from the Atlantic.

Magellan was assured by his mathematician friend Faleiro that this "South Sea," as it was called, could only be a couple of thousand miles across—scarcely wider than the Mediterranean was long. Moreover, according to Faleiro's calculations, the spice-rich Moluccas that lay across this sea would fall into the half of the world allotted to Spain by the 1494 Treaty of Tordesillas, which had divided the globe into Spanish and Portuguese halves. It was now clear to Magellan where his future fame and wealth lay—in finding a route around or through the New World to the Indies beyond. And if Portugal had spurned him, perhaps the Spanish Crown would not.

Magellan left Portugal and its ungrateful monarch behind forever in October 1517 and traveled to Seville, Spain's principal center of West Indian trade. There he was welcomed by Diogo Barbosa, a fellow Portuguese and a mariner who had been in the service of Spain for 14 years. But the Spanish were at first cool to Magellan's proposal. He went before the board of Seville's Casa de Contratacíon, the chamber responsible for Spain's colonial trade. Though vast profits might be reaped from the scheme, it appeared too risky to the board's conservative bureaucrats; it might involve fighting the Portuguese, and Spain was already beginning to take treasure out of the Americas. Nevertheless, as in Columbus' case, there was an individual whose vision—or greed—overcame his caution. Immediately after the official rejection, Magellan was approached by the board's chairman, Juan de Aranda, who confessed that he was most interested—as a private citizen. For a one-eighth share of the voyage's

King Charles I of Spain, Magellan's sponsor, wears the ornate necklace of the Order of the Golden Fleece, a Burgundian order of chivalry, in this 16th Century portrait, painted when Charles was 18.

profits, he offered to sponsor the project before the King's Council, a powerful body that could overrule the Casa de Contratacíon.

In January 1518 Magellan and his new wife—after a whirlwind courtship he had married Beatriz Barbosa, daughter of his host, Diogo Barbosa—along with the astronomer Faleiro, journeyed across Spain from Seville to Valladolid; there King Charles I, the grandson of Ferdinand and Isabella, was in residence with his council and the rest of his court. Of the council's four members, only one really counted: Juan Rodríguez de Fonseca, the crafty and powerful Bishop of Burgos.

The chronicler Bartolomé de Las Casas, who later wrote a monumental *Historia de las Indias*, described that historic council meeting. Magellan produced a painted leather globe that showed South America and his intended route down its east coast. He then proceeded to expound for the council on the wealth to be found in the East Indies. He produced a letter from an old comrade-in-arms named Francisco Serrão, who had reached the Moluccas and described their seductive riches. He also produced a Malay slave, Enrique, whom he had acquired years before in Malacca. Then his friend Faleiro demonstrated that, by his calculations, the Spice Islands must fall within Spain's share of the globe.

Magellan's presentation convinced Bishop Fonseca, and in short order the explorer found himself before King Charles. The monarch was only 18, but he was both shrewd and bold, and he enthusiastically backed Magellan's scheme. On March 22, 1518, Charles granted Magellan and Faleiro a contract. The King would provide five ships, with provisions and the money to hire crews. Magellan and Faleiro would become governors of any islands they found—and would be allowed a generous one fifth of the proceeds of their voyage. As fleet commander, Magellan was given the respected military title of captain general.

It was done. But for all the royal support, 18 months passed before the preparations were complete. This was an agonizing time for Magellan. The vessels he was given were scarcely worthy of the name and required extensive repairs—all of which was observed with great interest, and no little glee, by Portugal's inquisitive representative in Seville, Sebastião Alvarez. This spy identified the five ships selected for the voyage and watched as they were beached and careened in a Seville shipyard for their first overhaul in years. After the vessels were returned to the water for fitting-out, Alvarez went aboard them to have a close look for himself. Nobody stopped him as he roamed about above and below deck, reporting back to his king with satisfaction that they were deteriorating: "The ships of Magellan's fleet, Sire, are five; that is to say, one of a hundred and ten tons, two of eighty tons each, and the other two of sixty tons each, a little more or less. I went on board them a few times, and I assure your Highness that their frames are rotting to tinder."

Alvarez was particularly interested in the armament of the fleet, a subject of the greatest importance should Manuel decide to intercept Magellan and smash him at sea. Altogether the fleet mounted only 72 small guns, and Magellan's flagship, the *Trinidad*, was the only one to carry "four very good iron cannon." It was clear that should the opportunity arise, these impudent Spaniards would be easy prey for the crack gunners of the Portuguese squadrons patrolling the Indies.

Old and ill-armed vessels were only part of Magellan's troubles. He was also experiencing difficulty in rounding up proper crews. Though Spanish officials were perfectly willing to hire Portuguese seamen for most occasions, they complained that Magellan was employing too many of his countrymen for this journey. The authorities apparently feared that the Portuguese crewmen might turn their coats and give Portugal the fruits of the voyage. Magellan ended up with a wildly polyglot crew: Greeks, Germans, Italians, French, Flemings, Malays and Africans as well as Spaniards. And there were in the end, despite all grumbling, at least 37 Portuguese on the rolls. But Magellan was forced to sail with Spanish captains on three of his ships—Gaspar Quesada, Luis de Mendoza and Juan de Cartagena. These men would cause him great grief and very nearly wreck his expedition.

There was trouble, too, with Ruy Faleiro, the astronomer. Always of a suspicious nature, Faleiro became so obsessed with the idea that people were plotting to steal his and Magellan's plan and reach the Indies first that he became deranged. News of Faleiro's mental instability reached King Charles, and a few months before the fleet sailed he ordered Faleiro to remain in Seville—doubtless to Magellan's relief.

At last, on August 10, 1519, Magellan, his captains and his crewmen all attended a solemn Mass during which the captain general was ceremoniously given the royal standard, the flag of Spain, under which he would claim the lands he discovered in the name of King Charles. Then, accompanied by his slave Enrique, he went on board his flagship, the *Trinidad*, to begin one of history's epic voyages.

All too often the records of such journeys are incomplete and inaccurate, composed of recollection, surmise and perhaps, if history is fortunate, the dry gleanings from a ship's log. But Magellan had aboard his flagship a Venetian named Antonio Pigafetta, who was accepted as a member of the ship's company—not as an officer or crew member, but simply as an observer. He had approached Magellan, saying only that he had a thirst for adventure. He was a gentleman, a man of some means. Why he would—for no reward—expose himself to the dangers and hardships of so long a voyage has remained a mystery. One strong possibility is that Pigafetta was a spy in the employ of Venice. The Venetians resented mightily the inroads made on their eastern trade by Portugal—and it is reasonable to believe that they viewed this Spanish thrust with equal alarm and wanted an account of everything Magellan managed to discover. If that was the case—or even if there was cause for suspicion— why the shrewd Magellan went along with it is equally mysterious.

Whatever the motive for either man, Pigafetta kept a meticulous journal and recorded in brilliant detail much of what he saw on the voyage. He survived to return to Seville, and after he went home to Italy his journal was turned into a book. It is the most detailed and fascinating account of any of the great voyages of discovery.

Pigafetta's narrative begins on August 10, 1519, as Magellan's little flotilla of five ships—the *Trinidad, Santiago, San Antonio, Concepción* and *Victoria*—left the pier at Seville, hoisted sail and, their guns firing a noisy farewell, dropped down the Guadalquivir River toward the open

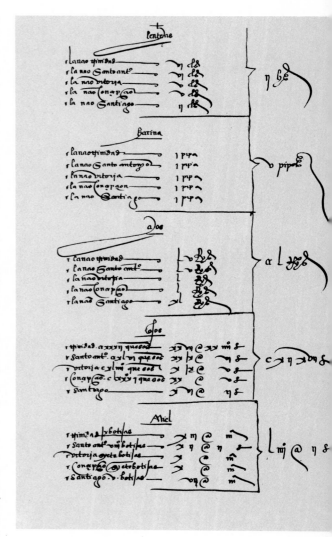

Meticulously penned and divided by commodity, ship and measure, this list details some of the provisions Magellan took on his voyage. The categories above and on the opposite page read, in order, "beans," "flour," "garlic," "cheese," "honey," "almonds," "anchovies," "sardines," "raisins" and "prunes." Magellan's five vessels are identified in the left column of each category, with the quantity of the foodstuff carried both by individual vessels and the fleet.

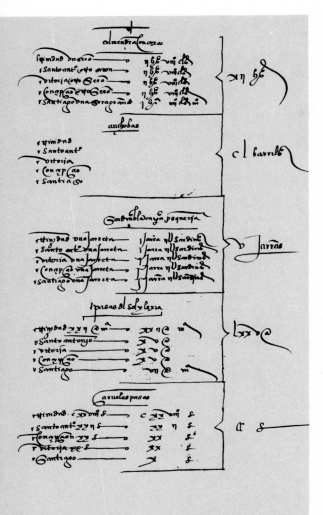

Magellan's appraisal of the comparative importance to health and morale, as well as the storage properties, of his provisions can be examined by converting the ancient measures inscribed in this ledger to modern units. The fleet carried only three bushels of beans and 800 pounds of flour, but took 250 strings of garlic buds, 2,817 pounds of cheese, 1,352 pounds of honey, one bushel of almonds, 150 barrels of anchovies, 10,000 sardines, 1,875 pounds of raisins and 200 pounds of prunes.

sea. Only a faint breeze was stirring. The vessels gained headway by use of the long wooden sweeps manned by seamen in the waist. Once the current caught them, the foresails were raised and the ships sailed slowly downstream in a single file.

The fleet traveled to the mouth of the river and halted at the small port of San Lúcar for more than two weeks to load supplies that the factors in Seville had unaccountably forgotten. Here the pious Magellan considerably annoyed his crews by forbidding them to have women on board for a last fling. Instead, he urged them to attend church every day, as he did.

They sailed into the Atlantic at last on September 20, 1519. Pigafetta noted that Magellan, before proceeding into the open sea, gave the other captains strict sailing orders to follow his flagship at all times and scrupulously observe any signals he might give. "To this end," Pigafetta wrote in his journal, "he carried by night on the poop of his ship a torch or burning fagot of wood, which they called a *farol*, that his ships should not lose him from sight." If Magellan showed two lights, it meant he was changing course, three meant reduce sail, and so forth.

It was a taut regime, requiring each ship to keep a lookout to catch the latest order from the flagship, and a touchy Spanish captain could easily feel his competence was being challenged. The Spanish also resented being led by a foreigner. "For the masters and captains of the other ships of his company," Pigafetta reported, "loved him not. I do not know the reason, unless it be that he, the captain general, was Portuguese, and they were Spaniards or Castilians, which peoples have long borne ill-will and malevolence toward one another."

To add to the tension, the explorers soon ran into contrary winds. There were fair winds for 15 days as the flotilla ran down the African coast. But then around Sierra Leone the ships were either becalmed or blown about by bafflingly light and variable winds for another 20 days.

"Sometimes we had the wind contrary," Pigafetta wrote, "at others fair, and rain without wind—which was very strange and uncommon, in the opinion of those who had sailed there several times before." Meanwhile, sharks dogged them: "During the calm great fish called *tiburoni* approached the ships. They have terrible teeth and eat men when they find them alive or dead in the sea."

The ominous calm was followed by a month of storms with blinding rain, and squalls so violent that the long yardarms on the mainmasts of the ships actually dipped into the water. Time and again, the vessels were on the verge of capsizing, and crewmen were frantically ordered to stand by with axes to chop down the masts if the ships were knocked on their beam-ends. All sails were struck and the fleet ran at the mercy of the gales under bare poles. The crews were terrified and despaired of survival—until, at the height of the tempest, the static electricity commonly seen on masts during such storms and called St. Elmo's fire appeared to reassure them. The saint, reported Pigafetta gratefully, "appeared in the form of a lighted torch at the height of the maintop, and remained there more than two hours and a half, to the comfort of us all. For we were in tears, expecting only the hour of our death." Whenever St. Elmo's fire appeared, Pigafetta concluded, "the ship never perishes."

Magellan might have avoided this weather had he chosen a different

Merchants and seamen congregate along the quays of Seville's Guadalquivir River, which teem with ships arriving and departing and in various stages of construction and refitting. Painted 50 years after Magellan assembled his fleet here, when Spain's thrust for empire was in full swing, this picture shows Seville as the center for exploration, and the richest and most populous city in the land. Towering above the city is the bell tower known as Giralda. The Cathedral of Seville, to its right, was one of the largest in the world. The Tower of Gold at the extreme right was used as the treasury for the riches that were returned from the Americas.

course. His route was south, barely out of sight of the African coast. The experience of almost a century of exploration in these waters had shown that to enter them was to ask for trouble. The name Sierra Leone, or Lion Mountain, had been given the area in 1462 by early Portuguese navigators because of its perpetually growling thunderstorms. Vasco da Gama as early as 1497 had avoided this part of the ocean by swinging far out into the Atlantic, and Magellan himself had been buffeted here by storms and head winds during his 1505 trip to India. Then why had he chosen this most uncomfortable course? The explanation may lie in the fact that he had been warned before leaving Seville that the Portuguese might try to intercept and destroy his Spanish expedition; he therefore chose a forbidding and unlikely course to avoid their warships.

"After we had passed the equinoctial line toward the south," Pigafetta noted, "we lost the North Star." Magellan and some of his Portuguese had been south of the equator before, but for the Spaniards, all familiar beacons were now behind them and an alien world lay ahead. With tempers already frayed by long calms and then vicious storms, it was not long before an open rupture occurred between Magellan and one of his Spanish captains. It was the custom each evening when the weather was good for each commander to approach in his ship, salute the captain general and ask if there were any orders. One evening the captain of the *San Antonio*, Juan de Cartagena, purposely omitted the captain general's proper title upon hailing the flagship. When Magellan reproached him, Cartagena insolently repeated the improper salute for two days.

On the fourth day Magellan called a meeting of the captains on his flagship. For once, the admirable Pigafetta failed to record what was said. He did note that Magellan had finally heard enough. Grabbing Cartagena by the front of his jacket, Magellan shouted, "You are my prisoner!" Cartagena yelled to the others to seize Magellan—but no one stirred. Magellan placed Cartagena under arrest and handed him over to Captain Luis de Mendoza of the *Victoria*. He then appointed Antonio de Coca, an experienced mariner and a relative of Bishop Fonseca, the new temporary captain of the *San Antonio*. Both Mendoza and de Coca were Spaniards, but for the moment at least they were loath to challenge Magellan. Nevertheless, their hearts were with Cartagena. Ill feeling continued to grow among the Spaniards, who increasingly resented taking orders from this tough little Portuguese.

And now Magellan abruptly changed course and sailed southwest across the Atlantic from the bulge of Africa to the bulge of Brazil. With fair winds the crossing took 70 days. His lookouts sighted Pernambuco—today's Recife—on November 29, and Magellan swiftly sailed south 2,000 miles along the Brazilian coast to the snug, almost landlocked bay of present-day Rio de Janeiro. Here the flotilla paused to take on water and fresh provisions.

The Guarani Indians were friendly and eager to barter with these strange visitors. The members of the expedition got some remarkable bargains, as Pigafetta reported. "The people of this place gave for a knife or a fishhook five or six fowles, and for a comb a brace of geese. For a small mirror or a pair of scissors they gave as many fish as ten men could have eaten." Pigafetta got the best bargain of all: "And for a king of

St. Elmo, patron saint of seamen, holds in his left hand a torch bearing his sacred fire, while with his other hand he cradles a carrack in whose tops dances the same eerie flame. In severe thunderstorms the appearance of this halo of static electricity, called St. Elmo's fire, was to sailors—Magellan's included—the sign that their heavenly guardian was on hand.

playing cards, of the kind used in Italy, they gave me five fowles, and even thought they had cheated me.''

The Indians, Pigafetta recorded, "sleep in nets of cotton, which they call in their language *Amache*"—the word has come down to us as hammock—and traveled in dugout canoes holding 30 or 40 men. The observant Pigafetta noted that "both men and women are in the habit of painting themselves with fire"—that is, tattooing—and went naked except for "a ring surrounded by the largest parrot feathers, with which they cover the part and backside only. Which is a very ridiculous thing.''

With horrified fascination, the chronicler described how the Indians "eat the flesh of their enemies, not as being good for food, but from custom. They do not eat the whole body of the man taken but eat it piece by piece. They cut him up in pieces, which they put to dry in the chimney, and every day they cut off a small piece and eat it with their ordinary food to call to mind their enemies.''

The explorers remained in Rio for almost two weeks, and then on December 26, well furnished with fresh provisions, Magellan's flotilla sailed out of the bay and cruised on down the coast for another 400 miles. Magellan noted that the coastline tended westward as well as south; he interpreted this as a sure sign that he would eventually find a strait leading west into the mysterious ocean Balboa had called the South Sea. Magellan joyously believed he had found the strait when he came upon a vast estuary, today known as the Rio de la Plata. But a two-day sail west along its course brought him to fresh water and disappointment: the "strait" was only a large river winding down to the Atlantic.

Magellan sent a well-armed landing party ashore to capture some of the Indians who had come down to the shore to gawk at the ships. But try as they might, his men were unable to capture a single Indian. The tall, fleet Indians easily outran the stumpy Europeans, for as Pigafetta noted, "they make more ground in one pace than we could in a leap.''

At this point in the voyage, Magellan and his navigators calculated that they were at lat. 35° S., more than 2,000 miles below the equator, deeper into the New World than any explorers had ever sailed before. The farther south they journeyed, the greater grew the fear and grumbling among the men, particularly the Spaniards. But Magellan pushed inexorably on. On February 3, 1520, he turned his back on a headland he had christened Monte Vidi—today's Montevideo—and headed down along the coast to a place he named Bahio de los Patos, literally Duck Bay. The explorers had found their first penguins—flightless birds of a species that one day would be called Magellanic penguins, the most northerly representatives of a family widely distributed through Antarctica. Pigafetta reported that "we loaded all the ships with them in a hour. And these goslings are black and have feathers over their whole body of the same size and fashion, and they do not fly, and they live on fish. And they were so fat that we did not pluck them but skinned them, and they have a beak like a crow's.''

It was now March, and the weather turned ominously colder as the Southern winter drew near. Still they sailed on, until they had reached a latitude "of 49½° toward the Antarctic Pole," as Pigafetta recorded. Here, on the afternoon of March 31, Magellan led his flotilla into a harbor

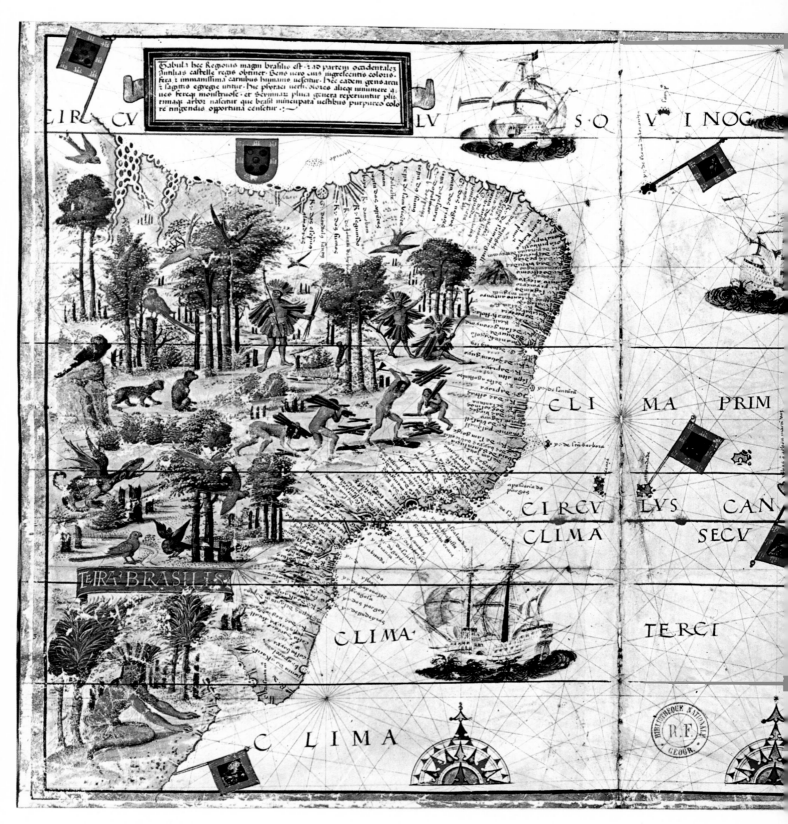

Feather-bedecked warriors, brilliant macaws, scampering monkeys and a dragon-like iguana inhabit the exotic land of Brazil in this 1519 Portuguese map. Based on reports from such early explorers as Cabral and Vespucci, it depicts the Brazilian coast between the Amazon River and the Río de la Plata and even includes lines of latitude marking the various climatic zones.

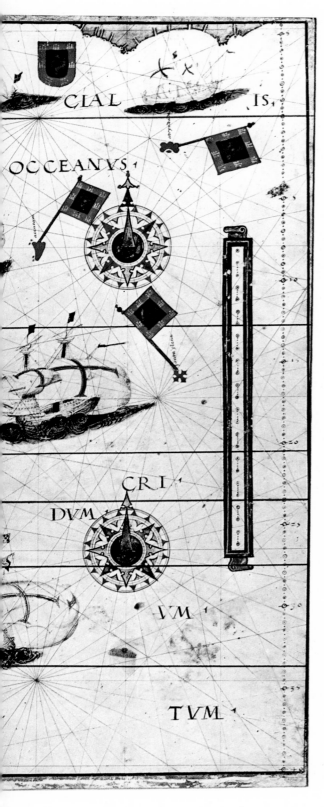

on the southern coast of today's Argentina; he named the place Port St. Julian. As soon as his ships were safely at anchor, Magellan announced to his officers and men that this cold, desolate, windy spot—more than halfway from the equator to the South Pole—would be their home for five months while they waited out the South American winter. He added that he was putting all hands on reduced rations.

There was an immediate clamor of protest. A spokesman for the crew angrily told Magellan that they had followed his commands for six long months, endured the savage storms of Africa, and had then crossed the Atlantic to a forsaken world that grew less and less hospitable the farther into it they penetrated. A number of men had already died from cold. They now believed Magellan was leading them all to their deaths. There was no passage from the Atlantic to the Indies. They would all perish on some icy rock. They demanded to return home.

But Magellan would not turn back. Endure the winter, he promised, and fame and wealth would be theirs.

Magellan's pledge stiffened the spines of many of the seamen. But it had no effect on five of his officers—all Spaniards—whose smoldering hatred for their Portuguese leader was about to burst into flame.

On the night of April 1, only a day after Magellan's speech, Gaspar Quesada, captain of the *Concepción*, with two of his officers and some 30 still-disaffected crewmen, stole aboard the *San Antonio*, surprising her Portuguese captain, Alvaro de Mesquita, and clapped him in irons. When the *San Antonio*'s second officer defied the mutineers, Quesada murdered him with furious stabs of his dagger. The mutineers speedily disarmed the rest of the crew, and the ship was theirs.

As all this was transpiring aboard the *San Antonio*, another Spaniard, Luis de Mendoza, captain of the *Victoria*, sided with the mutineers. At the same time, the insolent Juan de Cartagena, whom Magellan had arrested, was freed by the mutineers and put in command of the *Concepción*. When Magellan awoke in his flagship on the morning of April 2, three of his five ships were in the hands of rebellious officers. He remained in command only of his own *Trinidad* and the *Santiago*, the fleet's smallest vessel, captained by the Portuguese João Serrão, brother of one of Magellan's oldest friends.

It was by far the most desperate moment of a torment-filled journey that had already taken more than five times as long as Columbus' first voyage of discovery. The odds were strong that the mutineers would execute Magellan. At the very least, they would force him to sail back to Spain, a captive in chains certain to endure slander and disgrace, his great dream forever shattered.

Magellan responded to the threat with cool daring. Quesada afforded him his first opportunity to counterattack by sending a skiff across from the *San Antonio* bearing a letter demanding that they immediately set sail for Spain. Magellan agreed to a parley—on the *Trinidad*. Quesada, fearing a trick, sent the skiff back again with a refusal.

But now as the boat drew up to the *Trinidad*, on a side screened from the *San Antonio*'s view, Magellan ordered his men to seize the craft and imprison its oarsmen. He quickly put six of his own men, led by the fleet's chief marshal, Gonzalo Gomez de Espinosa, into the skiff; concealed in their clothes were long daggers. At the same time, Magellan ordered 15 more armed men into his own ship's boat, which also lay on the far side of the *Trinidad*, hidden from sight of the mutineers.

Rather than attack the *San Antonio* at once, Magellan decided to move first against Mendoza's *Victoria*. From the skiff, Espinosa waved a letter as his five companions rowed rapidly across the distance separating the two vessels. As they reached the *Victoria*, Mendoza allowed them to come alongside and clamber aboard. It was reported that Mendoza smiled derisively upon reading Magellan's letter, which summoned him to the flagship. If so, the mutineer's mirth was short-lived, for Espinosa, obeying Magellan's order, whipped out his hidden dagger and plunged it into Mendoza's throat. Espinosa and his followers were now in danger from the other mutineers aboard the *Victoria*. But hardly had the mortally wounded Mendoza fallen than the 15 men in the *Trinidad*'s boat arrived and swarmed over the *Victoria*'s side with muskets and swords. In the face of such strength, the *Victoria*'s mutineers surrendered.

With that, the advantage swung to Magellan, three ships to two, and as night fell, he ranged the *Victoria*, *Trinidad* and *Santiago* across the mouth of the harbor to block the remaining mutineers' escape. Soon after midnight, Quesada in the *San Antonio* bore down on Magellan's flagship as if to make a run for the open sea. As he drew near, Quesada shouted orders from the *San Antonio*'s quarter-deck for the crew to open fire. No one obeyed. On the *Trinidad*, Magellan gave the word, and the flagship's guns spewed flame. It only remained to send a boarding party to the *San Antonio* and place the hapless Quesada in chains.

Only the *Concepción* was left now and its temporary commander, Juan de Cartagena, surrendered the next morning.

Magellan's justice was swift and brutally instructive. Mendoza's body was taken ashore and accorded the ceremonial butchery meted out to traitors in the 16th Century, being hacked into four pieces. Quesada, who had murdered the mate of the *San Antonio*, was decapitated and also quartered. Juan de Cartagena, twice a mutineer, was not executed. Magellan condemned him to be marooned on the desolate Argentine shore when the flotilla departed; he was never seen or heard of again.

Magellan found 40 crewmen guilty of treason and sentenced them to death. But then, after allowing them to agonize briefly, he pardoned the lot, along with two officers who had taken minor parts in the uprising. It was brilliant psychology. Magellan's leniency turned the guilty men into devoted cohorts who would follow him to the ends of the earth—which is where Magellan took them.

Oddly, Antonio Pigafetta had very little to say of the mutiny, giving it only 11 lines in his narrative (the details are known from others on the voyage). Perhaps Pigafetta, who had come to admire Magellan deeply, felt the uprising reflected unfavorably on Magellan's leadership. At any rate, he had no doubts about the mutineers' intentions, writing that they conspired "against the captain general to bring about his death."

But if he played down the mutiny, Pigafetta had much to report about southern Argentina, which Magellan called Patagonia because the native Tehuelche Indians wore big leather boots (*patagón* means a large

The ocean beyond the isthmus

Attended by his comrades and a frisky canine, the overland explorer Balboa (inset) strides with sword and shield into the Pacific to claim the ocean for Spain.

When Ferdinand Magellan set sail from Spain on his historic voyage in 1519, he already knew that there was an ocean beyond the American land mass. Six years before, another Spanish explorer had penetrated overland from the Atlantic through the dark and steaming jungles of the Isthmus of Panama. He had emerged to gaze upon a great western sea and had claimed it for the Spanish Crown. This man was Vasco Núñez de Balboa, and he ranks as one of the more curious and appealing characters in the chronicles of discovery. He had no reputation as an explorer, no commission from king and queen, nothing in fact to point him to the task save the accidents of fate.

In 1501, at age 26, Balboa had shipped out to the New World, where he sought to make his fortune as a plantation owner in budding Hispaniola. But he had failed egregiously; to escape his dunning creditors, and weary of farming anyway, he had stowed away on a ship carrying colonists to Panama. Hiding in a large barrel, he emerged only when the vessel was well out to sea. Since an extra hand would be welcome in the trying times ahead, the expedition's commander accepted him as a member of the company.

In Darien, on the Isthmus of Panama, Balboa proved himself to be a handy fellow indeed, equally adept at thatching roofs or palavering with the colonists' Indian neighbors. He exhibited a certain air of leadership as well. In 1511, when the colony was established, the Governor appointed by King Ferdinand arrived to take command and demanded the gold the colonists had bartered from the Indians. With Balboa their elected head, the settlers chased the avaricious Governor back to his ship. In time, Balboa petitioned the Crown for permanent appointment as governor, listing among his qualities: "I have managed never to let my men go out of this place unless I go in advance, be the hour by night or by day, marching through rivers and marshes and woods and mountains."

But from Spain there was only silence. Balboa decided upon an act that could not fail to impress his sovereign. Hearing from the Indians that a great ocean lay across the isthmus, he gathered 190 Spaniards and 800 Indians, and on September 1, 1513, plunged into the jungles. Invaluable Indian guides and Balboa's own uncanny instinct steered them on a route that traversed the isthmus at a point a mere 50 miles wide. After 24 days, he and his men climbed the cool heights of a mountain; there in the distance, stretching to the horizon, lay the promised ocean.

Although Balboa's momentous discovery did earn him the title of Admiral of the South Sea, the King still denied him the governorship of Darien. The new governor, Pedro Arias de Avila, arrived there within months of Balboa's return, and even though the two coexisted in apparent harmony for several years, the Governor's jealousy of Balboa finally erupted. For his role in the earlier rebellion, Balboa was arrested on charges of treason, and quickly tried and convicted. On January 12, 1519, his severed head was impaled on a pole in the main square of Darien.

clumsy foot in Spanish). One day, Pigafetta reported, "we saw a giant who was on the shore, quite naked, and who danced, leaped and sang, and while he sang he threw sand and dust on his head." Magellan then "sent one of his men toward him, charging him to leap and sing like the other in order to reassure him and show him friendship. Which he did."

The Indian went trustingly aboard the flagship and amazed the mariners with his size; he might well have been seven feet tall. Now it was the Indian's turn to be astonished: "The captain caused the giant to be given food and drink, then he showed him other things, among them a steel mirror. Wherein the giant seeing himself was greatly terrified, leaping back so that he threw four of our men to the ground."

The comedy with the giant soon ceased when Magellan decided to capture two Patagonians as presents for King Charles—and, incidentally, as proof of his discoveries. First, a pair of these huge beings were invited on board by Magellan. "The means by which he kept them," Pigafetta explained, "was that he gave them many knives, scissors, mirrors, bells and glass, all which things they held in their hands. And meanwhile the captain sent for large iron fetters, such as are put on the feet of malefactors. Whereat the giants took great pleasure in seeing these fetters, and did not know where they had to be put, and they were grieved that they could not take them in their hands, because they were prevented by the other things aforesaid."

Magellan then made "signs that the fetters would be put on their feet. Whereat they made a sign with their heads that they were content with this. Forthwith the captain had the fetters put on the feet of both of them." When they perceived this trick, "they began to blow and foam at the mouth like bulls." They might well struggle; the cramped and squalid existence on the ships killed both of them before the year was out.

But the Indians were the merest of diversions. Halfway into the long, cold winter at Port St. Julian, Magellan sent the *Santiago*, commanded by João Serrão, probing down the coast. By May, Serrão had reached Puerto Santa Cruz. Then disaster. On May 22, the *Santiago* was wrecked, driven ashore in heavy weather. Only one man was drowned, but the 37 survivors were 70 miles from Magellan with no provisions.

For four days, Serrão and his men stumbled across the arid, windswept plains, until they reached the Rio de Santa Cruz. Here they would not starve, since the waters were teeming with fish. They built a small raft and Serrão sent two of his strongest men across the river with instructions to walk northward until they reached Magellan at Port St. Julian. It took the two men 11 days to make the 70-mile trek, and they arrived so battered and weary that their comrades scarcely recognized them. The relief party of 24 men, struggling across the wilderness in the dead of winter, somehow reached the *Santiago*'s men, and in another month all hands were miraculously safe back in Port St. Julian.

For his courage and fortitude, Serrão was rewarded with command of the *Concepción*, and now Magellan had trusted Portuguese as captains of all four of his vessels. Two of them were related to him: Duarte Barbosa, Magellan's brother-in-law, captained the *Victoria*, and Alvaro de Mesquita, a cousin, was in the *San Antonio*. Magellan felt himself ready to sail on as soon as the weather allowed.

It was now August, the beginning of the South American spring. Magellan shifted his fleet south to Puerto Santa Cruz, where the explorers spent another two months, "to supply ourselves," as Pigafetta recorded, "with water, wood and a kind of fish a cubit long and very scaly, and good to eat. Before departing thence, the captain general desired all to confess themselves and to receive the Body of our Lord, as good Christians." Then they were ready for one final push south to discover the long-sought strait—or to learn that it did not exist.

Magellan weighed anchor on October 18 and set sail. Three days later the fleet passed a high promontory. The seamen named it, in their devout fashion, the Cape of the Eleven Thousand Virgins. Behind it they spied the opening of an inlet, fringed on either side by jagged, snow-covered peaks. But there was little exultation aboard the vessels. The inlet looked forbidding, a funnel for screaming winds where the sounding lead found no bottom and the ships could secure themselves only to ropes made fast to the shore.

It was at this time that Magellan rose to his true stature as a leader. It may even be that the depths of his commitment to his mission had rendered him half-mad as he urged his men on, assuring them that this was indeed the strait that he had seen marked on a secret map in the Portuguese archives. It was a lie. However, it persuaded the command-

In a perspective looking south, with the Atlantic Ocean on the left and the entrance to the Pacific Ocean at right, this 17th Century engraving—complete with penguin and friendly Indians—illustrates the tortuous route that Magellan pursued between the oceans in 1520. The map commemorates the rediscovery of the Strait of Magellan by a Dutch fleet in 1615.

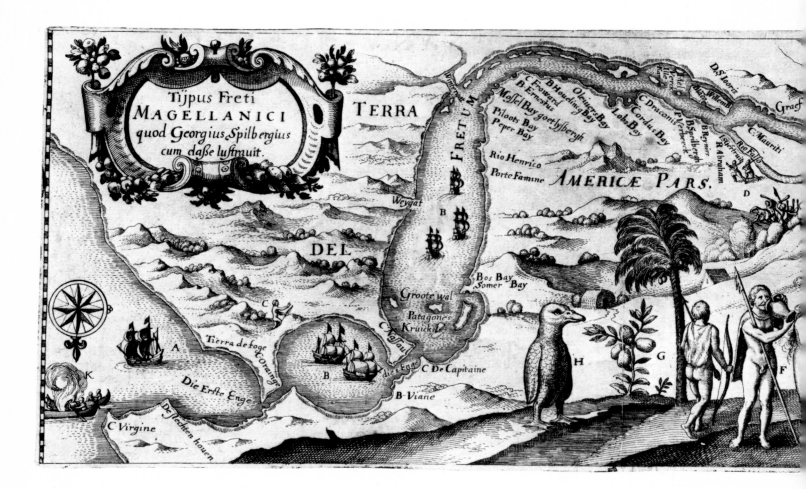

Thrusting an arrow down his throat to cure his stomach-ache, a Patagonian giant dwarfs a European man in this 1602 engraving. The first of these outsized tribesmen was sighted on the Argentine coast by Magellan's crew in 1520. "He was so tall," wrote Antonio Pigafetta, "that even the largest of us came only to midway between his waist and his shoulders."

ers of the *Concepción* and *San Antonio* to push ahead and reconnoiter.

The tension while the ships were gone and the relief at the news they brought back were vividly captured by Pigafetta: "Trying to return to us, they were hard put not to run aground. But approaching the end of the bay thinking themselves lost they saw a small opening, which did not seem an opening but a creek. And like desperate men they threw themselves into it, so that perforce they discovered the strait. Then seeing that it was not a creek but a strait with land, they went on, and found a bay. Then going further they found another strait, and another bay larger than the first two. Very joyful at this, they at once turned back to inform the captain general."

Magellan and those aboard the *Trinidad* and *Victoria* at first thought the other ships had perished in a great storm that raged about the inlet. Then "while in suspense," reported Pigafetta, "we saw the two ships approaching under full sail and flying their banners, coming toward us. When near us, they suddenly discharged their ordnance, at which we very joyously greeted them the same way. And then we all together, thanking God and the Virgin Mary, went foward."

Painfully and continually facing peril of shipwreck in the cramped seaway, Magellan's fleet started to feel its way along the strait. Zigzag creeks studded with islands, false inlets and dead ends made progress treacherous and slow. The fleet came at last across a definite fork in the channel, with one outlet to the southeast and the other outlet to the southwest. Once again Magellan divided up his fleet, taking the southwesterly fork with the *Trinidad* and *Victoria* and leaving the other to the *Concepción* and *San Antonio*.

After probing a short distance, Magellan anchored to reconnoiter. "We sent a boat well furnished with men and provisions to discover the cape of the other sea. They spent three days going and returning, and told us that they had found the cape and the great and wide sea. Wherefore the captain, for the joy that he had, began to weep and gave this cape the name Cape of Desire, as a thing much desired and long sought."

But crushing news was waiting for Magellan as he withdrew to the rendezvous to tell the other captains to call off the search. The *San Antonio*—the biggest ship in the fleet, carrying most of the stores of food—had vanished. Magellan sent the *Victoria* right back to the Atlantic end of the strait in search of wreckage or survivors. No trace was found. The *Victoria*'s crew left a marker flag and a message in hopes that the *San Antonio* might return to the strait and try to regain contact. At last, Magellan was forced to acknowledge that the *San Antonio*'s officers must have decided to desert.

For the moment, only one course was open to Magellan. The best possible way to answer any lies that the *San Antonio* deserters might tell about him back in Spain would be to complete the voyage in triumph and return with witnesses to the true facts. Out to the west the open expanse of the South Sea pointed the way to the Spice Islands. Magellan never hesitated. It was with the true sense of history in the making that Pigafetta recorded how "on Wednesday the twenty-eighth of November, one thousand five-hundred and twenty, we issued forth from the said strait and entered the Pacific Sea."

That unique, that most famous ship, the "Victoria"

In early October, 1518, five old and weather-worn ships struggled up the Guadalquivir River to the shipyards of Seville; at times the decrepit vessels had to be towed by men in rowboats. A Portuguese diplomat sent to spy on the little Spanish fleet in which Magellan would try to sail to the Indies described the ships as "very old and patched. I would not care to sail to the Canaries in such old crates."

It was not surprising that explorers sailed in second-rate vessels; their missions were usually shoestring ventures considered too risky for a fine new nao or caravel.

As it was, Magellan was shortchanged on the price for his derelicts. Altogether, the fleet cost 1.5 million maravedis. That would have been a reasonable enough sum for five vessels in good condition. But it took Magellan all of 18 months to repair and refurbish the ships, and in the end, he wound up spending another two million maravedis.

Throughout this frustrating delay, Magellan supervised the small army of shipwrights who swarmed over the hulls tearing out old planking, replacing braces, recaulking, stepping new masts and rigging with new lines and sails.

Once seaworthy, the ships were loaded with trade goods and provisions and equipped with weapons for defense: 62 cannon, 10 smaller guns called falconets, which fired scrap shot, and scores of swords, pikes and crossbows. For trading, there was a curious assortment of goods: 20,000 hawks' bells, 500 pounds of glass beads, cotton and wool cloth, fishhooks, and 400 dozen German knives, candidly described in ships' accounts as "of the worst quality."

There were ample stores of the basics: 10 tons of biscuit, 6,000 pounds of salt pork and 500 butts of wine. Magellan also allotted four boxes of quince jelly to each vessel—save for the flagship, which was blessed with 35 boxes.

But for all the provisioning and refitting, only the *Victoria* completed the awesome circumnavigation. "That unique, that most famous ship, the *Victoria*," contemporary chronicler Gonzalo Fernández de Oviedo described her—and justly so, for after her epic voyage the *Victoria* completed three Atlantic crossings before she was lost at sea in 1525 returning from Hispaniola in the New World.

Careened on the bank of the Guadalquivir River in Seville in 1518, the Victoria is held firmly in place by lines running from the mainmast to capstans anchored onshore. She has been bared virtually to her frames as shipwrights fit her with tough new oaken planking. At the bow, workmen seal the new planking with a mixture of pitch and horsehair, while yardmen aft hoist a new rudder into place. Facing the Victoria on the bank, the Santiago, her hull repairs complete, is being rerigged as seamen haul a new sail into the tops. Near the carpenters' sheds at the far right, workmen construct a new skiff for the Trinidad.

At the ropewalk, workers girdled by fibrous bundles of hemp attach the fiber to revolving hooks on man-powered spinning machines, at center, and then walk slowly backward, paying out the hemp as it twists into rough yarn. To make the long yarn needed for lengthy marine cables, ropemakers sometimes retreated hundreds of yards, slipping the yarn through overhead and waist-high guides like those at left, to keep it off the ground. When all the fiber had been paid out, the yarn was reeled back in on spools, at right, and then carried off to be saturated in weatherproofing tar before being spun into finished rope.

To spin the hemp into strong, durable rope, workers at the ropewalk maintain a clockwise twist in three separate strands at left, while at right workers bind all three strands together by twisting them in the opposite direction. This use of opposite twists counteracted the rope's natural tendency to unwind. Because

the rope shortened slightly with every twist, the big binding crank and the center guide were mounted on heavy sleds to enable them to move slowly with the inevitable contraction.
Between the sleds, workers use staves to add leverage to the twist, in order to ensure that the bind is both tight and uniform.

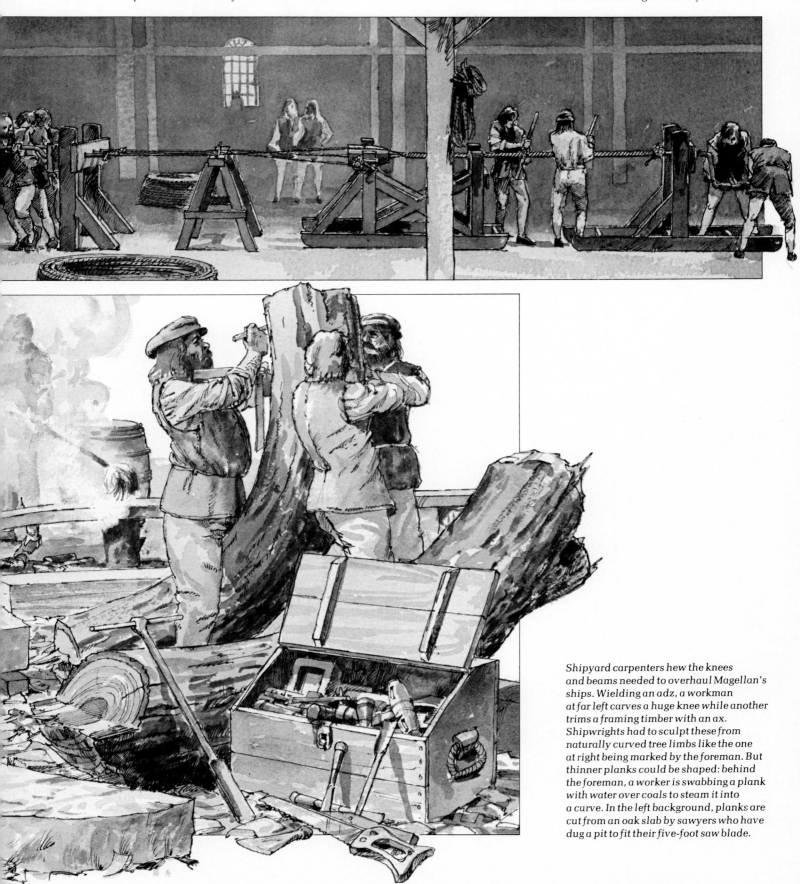

Shipyard carpenters hew the knees and beams needed to overhaul Magellan's ships. Wielding an adz, a workman at far left carves a huge knee while another trims a framing timber with an ax. Shipwrights had to sculpt these from naturally curved tree limbs like the one at right being marked by the foreman. But thinner planks could be shaped: behind the foreman, a worker is swabbing a plank with water over coals to steam it into a curve. In the left background, planks are cut from an oak slab by sawyers who have dug a pit to fit their five-foot saw blade.

At dockside after fitting out, the Victoria takes on an array of provisions, including a cow bellowing in protest as she is lowered into the hold. On the quay near the bow, other supplies are stockpiled for loading: seamen's chests, rope, cooking kettles, oil jars, anchors and a small arsenal of cannon and pikes.

Beneath the Victoria's stern, workmen fill sandbags for ballast and load them aboard through an aft port. Casks of food and trade goods are unloaded from carts, one cask so clumsily that it breaks open (foreground). Firewood for the ship's cookstove awaits loading, and four stevedores team up to shoulder a water barrel.

The Santiago, tied up astern of the Victoria, is loaded with her share of stores, some of which are being lowered from the loft of the warehouse at right. Standing on the dock near two ships' boats and bales of cloth for trading, a shipboy totes the drum and tambourines that will be used to entertain the crew on the voyage.

In mid-ocean aboard the Victoria, a shipboy taps out a merry rhythm on his tambourine while crewmen gather around a portable wood-burning cookstove for the midday meal—a seaman's stew of fish or long-simmered salted meat, their only hot food of the day. This humble fare, and a ration of durable biscuits, was washed down with watered wine. Old canvas scraps were spread like picnic blankets on the deck. To minimize the risk of fire—a constant concern on wood ships—the stove was placed against the lee rail, and a bucket of water was kept on hand.

Legs braced against the pitch of the ship, the helmsman leans into the Victoria's heavy tiller as a crewman on the ladder relays orders for course changes from an officer on deck. In front of the helmsman at the binnacle, where the compasses and other vital nagivational aids were housed, one seaman records the ship's heading on a slate while another turns the sandglass. At left, weary sailors, who had no sleeping quarters, huddle in exhaustion between watches.

Fighting for their lives in a raging Atlantic gale, the crewmen of the Victoria, having lowered the main yard, scramble to shorten sail. As the vessel heels over precariously on a rolling ocean wave, one bold seaman in the bow crawls out onto a swaying yardarm to secure the foresail with gaskets.

RICHARD SCHLECHT

An officer on the quarter-deck roars out orders to the crew while two sailors nearby wrestle a watertight canvas cover over a hatchway. Aft on the poop deck, the topside binnacle with its precious contents of navigational instruments has been lashed securely to the deck rings, and its brass latch made fast.

Clinging for dear life to the weather rail as the deck surges underfoot, a seaman keeps a sharp eye on Magellan's flagship, the Trinidad, as she runs before the wind on the heaving seas. Half hidden by monstrous swells, the Trinidad's battered mainsail still bears intact the cross of St. James, a patron saint of Spain.

Chapter 5

The death and the triumph of Magellan

believe that nevermore will any man undertake such a voyage." Thus did the chronicler Antonio Pigafetta sum up Magellan's greatest achievement: Western man's first conquest of the Pacific Ocean.

It was, to begin with, a matchless feat of endurance: 98 days and 13,000 miles across the mightiest ocean on the planet, an ocean whose true size had never been remotely envisaged. No seafarers in history ever had to go so long without fresh food and water, without setting foot on dry land. In crossing the unknown Pacific, Magellan and his men contributed more knowledge of the world's geography than any single sea voyage had ever achieved. The crossing proved that the Pacific Ocean, not the Eurasian land mass, was the world's biggest natural feature, and it showed at last that ships, as the medieval storyteller Sir John Mandeville had blithely proclaimed in his ignorance 150 years before, could indeed "go all about the world."

A log of the voyage painstakingly kept by Francisco Albo, a pilot in the fleet, shows that Magellan steered northward for 23 days after leaving the strait, staying as far out to sea as possible without completely losing sight of the South American coastline. While the ships drove northward, Pigafetta and the crewmen were entertained by the albacores and bonitos, "which pursue other fish called *colondrini*"—flying fish, from the Spanish word for a swallow, *golondrina*. These flying fish, Pigafetta noted, "spring from the water and fly about a bowshot—so long as their wings are wet and then regain the sea. Meanwhile their enemies follow their shadow, and arriving at the spot where they fall, seize upon them and devour them—a thing marvelous and agreeable to see."

The sea hissed under the sides of the vessels when the wind was right, and in a little more than three weeks the ships made some 1,600 miles. By December 19 they were fast approaching lat. 30° S. opposite north-central Chile, a warm enough latitude for comfortable sailing. Magellan began to edge out from the coast, steering northwest on December 19, 20 and 21. Then, on December 22, he turned away from the jagged Chilean coastline and headed into the high Pacific.

In his eagerness to get started across the Pacific, Magellan had made a grave error by not putting into one harbor or another for fresh water and provisions. He had no idea of the size of the Pacific—the distance was more than a third of the earth's circumference. And because of this ignorance, compounded by carelessness, the voyage became one of the most appalling ordeals in the annals of the sea.

The crossing began quite cheerfully. As the ships scudded farther and farther away from land on a splendid following wind, the daily run became impressive; "by this wind," Pigafetta noted, "we made each day fifty or sixty leagues or more." In addition, the ships were being aided by a following current, the South Equatorial Drift, flowing due west.

Wind and current were thus on Magellan's side, but by mid-January he had two looming worries. He had sailed more than 3,000 miles since leaving the Chilean coast and not a speck of land had he found. His second concern was ominously linked to the first. Unless they found land soon, every crew member would die of starvation or scurvy.

"The captain, knowing that the wooden image greatly pleased the queen, gave it to her," wrote Magellan's chronicler Pigafetta of this doll-like statue of the Christ Child. Before giving her the figure, Magellan had converted the wife of the Sultan of Cebu to Christianity. The 13-inch statue, the first Christian image venerated in the Philippines, remains the oldest artifact of the Spaniards' arrival.

Magellan decided to change course and headed northwest toward the equator. He knew from the Portuguese that the Moluccas were just south of the equatorial line. Sailing directly west on their latitude would shorten the voyage. It was a fateful decision. Had Magellan held to his more southerly course, he would have come across the atolls and islands of the southern Tuamotu Archipelago and discovered Tahiti. There he would have found all the fresh provisions any crew could desire.

The new course would have taken Magellan near the smaller Marquesas Group but for the fact that his lookouts, on January 21, spotted a towering cumulus cloud, a sign of land. Magellan now headed southwest, searching for this land—and found only Pukapuka, a tiny island washed by swift currents and surrounded by water too deep to anchor. Thus Magellan, having steered north of Tahiti, now steered south of the Marquesas, missing them and their supplies of food and water.

Totally unaware of how close they had come to paradise on earth, the explorers sailed on into a living hell. By the end of January, starvation and disease were daily strengthening their grip on the three crews. Pigafetta spent only a few hundred words on their plight, but his description is nonetheless harrowing: "we remained three months and twenty days without taking on board provisions or any other refreshments, and we ate only old biscuit turned to powder, all full of worms and stinking of the urine that the rats had made on it, having eaten the good. And we drank water impure and yellow. We ate ox hides, which were very hard because of the sun, rain and wind." They also ate sawdust and rats—which the stronger members of the crew captured and sold to the weaker. Pigafetta wrote that the noisome beasts brought "half an écu apiece."

On the face of it, Magellan's men, with their record of dissatisfaction and mutiny, should have rebelled violently against such privations. But they did not. What kept them going was the hope that any day the yearned-for Spice Islands would be sighted—a hope that could only have been kept alive by the iron confidence of their leader. In any case, the men were now too sick to turn back.

Grimly entering the daily course and position in his log, the pilot Francisco Albo had no time to record the crew's afflictions. But the course he recorded for the first two weeks of February spoke of the desperate plight the men were in. Magellan was now steering northwest, driving for the equator as directly as he dared without losing the advantage of the following wind.

Eleven days after leaving Pukapuka they made a second landfall: another uninhabited islet. Here they were forced to stop and fish, but they found little profit in it. The waters swarmed with sharks. With no hope of capturing food fish in the midst of the circling pack, the men fished for the sharks themselves. It was perilous business, and they gave the place the name Tiburones, or Shark Island. Tiburones was probably Caroline Island, 700 miles west of the Marquesas.

As he drove his dying crews northwest toward the equator, Magellan could only hope that Tiburones might turn out to be the most southeasterly outpost of the Moluccas. But after holding steadily northwest for another agonizing week and crossing the equator, he found that the horizon remained stubbornly empty. Unbelievable as it seemed, considering the length of the voyage, the Moluccas clearly lay still farther west.

Magellan dared not steer for them directly, though. Fifty years of experience on the African route had taught Portuguese seafarers to avoid the equator with its leaden calms and violent electrical storms. He would get north of the equator and hope to pick up an equivalent wind to the easterlies that had been carrying Spanish ships across the Atlantic since 1492. Albo's list of daily latitudes shows that it took 14 days to climb to 13° N. after crossing the equator, a latitude Magellan believed might take him to a landfall on the coast of Japan. He now turned straight west and held course, the only time in the voyage that he followed a latitude line for six days. It was indicative of his plight. The crews were too weak to try any fancy sailing; they were running west along lat. 13° with the wind at their backs, unable to do more. This was Magellan's last throw, the seafarer's equivalent of a forced march.

Then his luck changed. On March 6, 1521, the outlying atolls of the Mariana Islands rose over the western horizon. There was no time for the crews to relax as they anchored off Guam. The islanders swarmed out in their canoes and tried to steal everything not nailed down: "the people of those islands entered the ships and robbed us so that we could not protect ourselves from them," wrote Pigafetta. Albo's log adds that their canoes "ran so, that they seemed to fly, and they had mat sails of a triangular shape, and they went both ways, for they made of the poop the prow, and of the prow the poop, as they wished."

Magellan was infuriated when these artful thieves managed to steal his ship's boat, which had been lowered into the water preparatory to going ashore; the islanders slipped under the *Trinidad*'s stern, cut the boat's hawser and towed it away. Driven past endurance, Magellan ordered crossbow men to the rails to shoot every canoeist within range.

The crossbow bolts took a terrible toll, especially because the islanders when shot drew the shafts out, leaving gaping wounds. As Pigafetta noted with astonishment, "whenever we wounded any of those people with a shaft that entered their body, they looked at it and then marvelously drew it out, and so died forthwith."

Magellan was still not content: he demanded the boat back. Ships' boats were vital during voyages in unknown waters. Boats could venture into shallows and row safely about, taking soundings, or go ashore for supplies. So Magellan combed all three ships for every able-bodied man and took an armed party, 40 strong, ashore on a punitive expedition.

Most of the islanders were still in their canoes, and only seven were killed as the landing party stormed through the settlement to which the stolen longboat had been towed. Before Magellan's men set the wood and palm-matting huts on fire, they swept them clean of food—coconuts, sweet potatoes and flying fish.

The explorers had no further trouble with the islanders, but Magellan was determined to press ahead. The men now had only a week's easy sailing without a single change of course before land was sighted again on March 16: the island of Samar in the Philippines.

When Magellan saw Samar loom up ahead, he knew he had not yet arrived at the Moluccas—this new landfall was too far north. But he had to give his men time to rest and recover before going on. The next part of the voyage might well be the most trying of all. The Portuguese had known where Magellan's fleet was bound before it even sailed; warships would surely be waiting to stop it from reaching the Moluccas. Even if Magellan found the Moluccas, loaded his ships with precious spices and then got away, most ports and trading stations on the route back to Spain would be Portuguese outposts and closed to him. To avoid these, the trip home would have to be a nonstop voyage as long as the Pacific crossing. Before they so much as approached the Moluccas, every man must be fighting fit and the ships stocked full for the homeward run.

Magellan therefore chose an unobtrusive anchorage when he arrived in the eastern Philippines: the uninhabited little island of Homonhon, at the mouth of Leyte Gulf. Some of the crew went ashore on March 17 to pitch tents for those who were sick. Two excellent fresh-water springs were quickly found, and for the first time in four months every man in the fleet reveled in the luxury of unlimited clean, clear water—intoxicating after the stinking gruel of algae in the ships' water casks. And each day, Pigafetta noted, Magellan made the rounds of his sick men and personally gave them coconut milk, "which greatly refreshed them."

Philippine islanders did not put in an appearance until the day after Magellan's flotilla dropped anchor. When they did, Pigafetta reported, "forthwith the most ornately dressed of them went toward the captain general, showing that he was very happy at our coming. Then the captain, seeing that these people were reasonable, ordered that they be given food and drink, and he presented to them red caps, mirrors, combs, bells and other things. And when those people saw the captain's fair dealing, they gave him fish and a jar of palm wine, figs more than a foot long, and other smaller ones of better flavor, and two coconuts." What was more, they indicated that they would return in four days with more coconuts, rice and other food.

On the 22nd the islanders proved as good as their word, coming back not only with two laden canoes but also with their chief and his entourage, all glittering with gold earrings, bracelets and arm bands. But where Columbus would have made no secret of his delight in the gold, Magellan refrained from any great show of interest. Instead he maintained the stance of a leader of peaceful men who had come to the islands in friendship and would accept nothing without a fair exchange. None of the other explorers behaved toward native peoples with such fairness.

After an eight-day rest on Homonhon, most of the sick were well on the way to recovery, and Magellan decided that it was time to probe deeper into the archipelago and find the overlord of the islands. A three-day cruise through the islets in the Surigao Strait brought them to anchor at the island of Limasawa on March 28, Holy Thursday, and here Magellan decided to spend the Easter weekend.

Initial contact with the inhabitants of Limasawa was also successful. The local ruler himself had rowed out to inspect the ships. Communication was easy because it developed that Enrique, Magellan's Malay slave for the past 10 years, could understand the Tagalog language and the Filipinos could understand his. "The captain made good cheer to those who came to the ship and gave them many things," Pigafetta related.

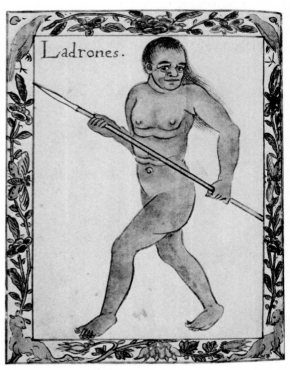

"They have long hair down to their waist, they go quite naked," wrote Antonio Pigafetta to describe the warriors of the Ladrones. His observation is confirmed by this 16th Century illustration.

Members of the Visayan culture on Cebu and Samar in the Philippines fascinated Magellan's crews. Pigafetta described them as tawny, short and fat— and covered with "diverse patterns."

"Wherefore the king wished to give the captain a bar of massy gold, of a good size, and a basket full of ginger. But the captain, thanking him greatly, refused to accept the present."

Far from taking offense at having his gift handed back, the chief— called Rajah Calambu—was pleased and invited Magellan to anchor off his village. On the following morning, Good Friday, Magellan sent Enrique ashore with a formal request to purchase provisions for money, telling the rajah that "he had come into his country, not as an enemy, but as a friend," as Pigafetta related. This time Rajah Calambu brought the *Trinidad* token gifts of food: "three porcelain jars covered with leaves and full of rice." Magellan returned the compliment by presenting to Rajah Calambu a fine "robe of red and yellow cloth, made in the Turkish fashion, and a very fine red cap." Then Magellan completely won the rajah over by asking if he would consent to become his blood brother in the Malay ceremony of *casicasi*, with both parties cutting their wrists and letting their blood mingle. Rajah Calambu delightedly agreed.

And now Magellan dazzled his new blood brother with an explosive display of Spanish power. The trade goods were shown and inspected and then some of the ship's guns were fired. The rajah was "greatly astonished" by the gunfire, Pigafetta solemnly noted, but not nearly so astonished as when Magellan presented a Spaniard in armor, immune from the swords and daggers with which three men were striking him.

Magellan played an even more impressive card on Easter Sunday, March 31. He ordered a public Mass to be said ashore and sent Enrique ahead to invite Rajah Calambu and his brother Rajah Siaiu, ruler of the Leyte Gulf islands, to attend.

Magellan landed with a party of 50 men, all dressed in their best and carrying their swords. As the boats neared shore, a six-gun salute was fired by the ships in honor of the two rajahs, who were waiting on the beach. Magellan walked between them to the place prepared for the saying of Mass, sprinkling them with scented water. They did not join in the offertory but copied Magellan in the rest of the service, going on their knees with raised hands at the elevation of the Host. With a showman's eye for maximum effect, Magellan had arranged for all the guns in the ships to fire when this solemn moment came.

After communion and Mass, Magellan opened the Easter celebrations with a fencing display by his men before getting down to business. "He had a cross brought," wrote Pigafetta, "with the nails and the crown to which those kings did reverence. And the captain caused them to be told that these things that he showed them were the insignia of the Emperor his lord and master, by whom he was charged and commanded to set them up in all the places where he should go and travel. And he told them that he wished to set them up in their country for their benefit, so that if any ships of Spain came afterward to those islands, they seeing the said cross would know that we had been there. And by this token they would do them no harm, and if they took any of their men, being immediately shown this sign, they would let them go." The rajahs thanked the captain "and said that they would be willing to do this."

Having obtained this welcome concession so easily, Magellan made it clear that he needed provisions for his ships. He also stated, however,

A priceless record of an epic voyage

By his splendid narrative of the first circumnavigation, the Venetian Antonio Pigafetta shares in the grandeur of Magellan's voyage. This bust shows him some years later, at about the age of 40.

Ferdinand Magellan's circumnavigation produced not just a new passage to the Indies, but also a wealth of information. Wonderful accounts of the voyage were brought back by all the survivors, but principally by the Italian chronicler Antonio Pigafetta.

The process by which Pigafetta's story circulated reveals a great deal about communication in Renaissance Europe. Soon after the *Victoria's* return to Seville on September 8, 1522, Pigafetta gave King Charles I "a book treating of all the things that had occurred on our voyage." A month later, in a letter home, the Mantuan Ambassador reported that he had seen the volume, and called it "very beautiful."

Pigafetta himself journeyed to both France and Italy, where he related his adventures to key figures. He next prepared a second manuscript, this one for his patron, the grand master of the Order of St. John of Jerusalem. Both manuscripts later vanished and Pigafetta's priceless journal would have been lost to history had there not been a considerable number of hand-crafted copies, four of which—one in Italian, three in French—survive.

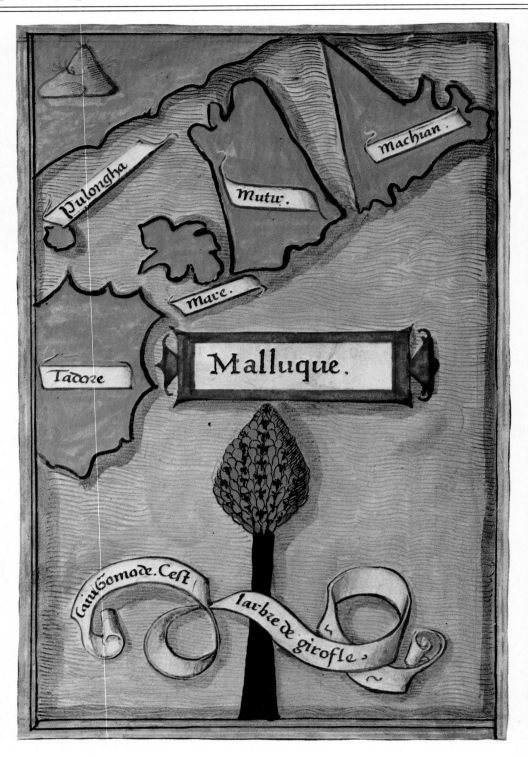

Copied from Pigafetta's illustrations, this drawing for a French version of his manuscript shows the four main spice-growing islands of the Moluccas, with a stylized rendering of the coveted clove tree.

Based on another illumination made
by Pigafetta, this rendering of the Ladrones,
oriented with south at the top, illustrates
the lateen-sailed outriggers that impressed
Magellan with their sailing ability.

that he had no intention of stripping Limasawa bare but would seek a bigger island, one with ample food resources. After an evening banquet on the shore, the rajahs offered Magellan the services of pilots to guide him to Cebu, where he might be able to obtain his supplies. The captain general accepted and "promised to treat them like himself, and that he would leave one of his men as a hostage." But Rajah Calambu waved this suggestion aside: "For love of him he wished to go himself to guide him to those ports and be his pilot," wrote Pigafetta, if Magellan would wait two days until the rajah had managed to harvest his rice. Magellan agreed and even sent some of his own men to help with the harvest.

Compared with the arrogant and greedy behavior of Spanish and Portuguese pioneers elsewhere, Magellan's handling of the Easter negotiations on Limasawa was remarkable for its tolerance and restraint. He proved to all that he was much more than a steel-willed leader of men, a peerless seaman and navigator: he could, when required, show the sensitivity and courtesy of a born diplomat.

The *Trinidad, Victoria* and *Concepción* sailed for Cebu on April 3, with Rajah Calambu as an honored passenger. When they arrived three days later at the island, they found a very different ruler from the easygoing lords of the outer islands. While he welcomed the explorers and fellow rajah, the estimable Calambu, Rajah Humabon of Cebu announced that it was customary for all vessels arriving in his country to pay tribute. Only four days before, he said, a ship had come from the kingdom of Siam and had duly paid a tribute of gold and slaves.

Enrique politely but firmly told the rajah that Magellan served the most powerful ruler in the world, who paid tribute to no other; the ships of Spain had come in peace, but if Cebu wanted war, war she could have. At this tense moment the Siamese merchant broke in and excitedly addressed Rajah Humabon in a speech Pigafetta thought worth preserving: "Have good care, O king, what you do, for these men are of those who have conquered Calicut, Malacca and all India the Greater. If you give them good reception and treat them well, it will be well for you, but if you treat them ill, so much the worse it will be for you, as they have done at Calicut and at Malacca." Enrique then added, Pigafetta noted, that if Rajah Humabon did not treat his subjects well, the King of Spain would send "so many men against him that he would destroy him."

Confronted with this daunting prospect, Humabon played for time, saying that he must consult his council. For his part, Magellan decided to reduce the tension by bringing the negotiations down to the level he preferred: exchanges of gifts and courtesies, and personal contact on friendly terms. The next day was spent in assuring Humabon that the Christian emperor expected no tribute, and in accepting Humabon's offer of blood brotherhood. Magellan also made a little speech that Pigafetta recorded, saying that "our weapons were mild to our friends and sharp to our enemies, and that, just as linen absorbs a man's sweat, so our weapons destroy the enemies of our faith."

This was flowery language for another veiled threat of force, but it was effective. On the following day, Humabon sent out his nephew and heir at the head of a formal delegation, which Magellan received enthroned on his flagship in a red velvet chair with his officers ranked behind him.

Magellan's murder on Mactan Island is depicted in this engraving published by German historian Levinus Hulsius in 1603. While tribesmen at the bottom peacefully trade fruit with Magellan's ships, on another part of the island, naked warriors armed with clubs and bows assault Magellan—holding a sword and shield— and his pike-wielding crew. Actually, the battle was waged just off the beach.

The prince and his party explained that they had come to arrange peace between Humabon and Magellan: The rajah even agreed to a Christian baptism—which Magellan happily arranged at a splendid public ceremony, christening Humabon "Don Charles" and the prince "Don Ferdinand" after Charles I of Spain and his brother. Within eight days, virtually the whole of Cebu had been converted to the faith.

So encouraged was Magellan by this missionary success that he took the tremendous risk of having his chaplain baptize a sick man, promising an immediate cure. By incredible good fortune, the man revived at once and was up and walking within five days. Now, to the islanders, Magellan was the miracle-working prophet capable of any triumph. Perhaps he believed it himself. This mantle of invincibility in which he seemed cloaked would soon prove his undoing.

On Friday, April 26, 1521, there came to Cebu a chief named Zula, one of two leaders jockeying for the lordship over the neighboring island of Mactan. Zula swore allegiance to Humabon and to Magellan but asked for help against his rival Lapulapu, who fiercely refused to recognize the authority of Humabon.

Magellan could hardly refuse Zula's appeal: he had talked too much about the invulnerability of his armed crewmen, and about their consequent value to friendly rulers. So he organized a force of 60 men and prepared to lead them against Lapulapu's men. "We besought him not to come," lamented Pigafetta, "yet he, as a good shepherd, would not abandon his sheep." The ships sailed from Cebu at midnight on the 26th.

Anchoring off Mactan three hours before dawn on the following day, Magellan sent an emissary ashore with a promise of friendship to Lapulapu in exchange for allegiance to the King of Spain. Back came the reply: Lapulapu feared not the Christians, having "lances of bamboo hardened in the fire and stakes dried in the fire." The Spaniards could attack when they pleased.

First light on April 27 revealed an unappealing prospect. The town ruled by Lapulapu stood on a bay whose rock-studded waters were too shallow to allow the ships to sail in close and bombard the shore with their cannon. The water was even too shallow for the ships' boats to approach the beach. The explorer and 49 of his men had to go over the side and wade across the bay for 600 or 700 yards to reach the shore.

Magellan and his men had hardly reached shore when they were attacked by 1,500 resolute warriors. Magellan then tried the tactic that had panicked the islanders on Guam: burning the huts. But this only further angered Lapulapu's warriors, who came howling down to destroy the invaders. Magellan's men cowered under a hail of missiles—rocks, spears and arrows—and he shouted for them to withdraw to the boats. Pigafetta, who was fighting close to his hero and had his forehead gashed by an arrow, described what followed: "He ordered us to withdraw slowly, but the men fled while six or eight of us remained with the captain. And those people shot at no other place but our legs, for the latter were bare. Thus for the great number of lances and stones they threw and discharged at us we could not resist. Our large pieces of artillery that were in the ships could not help us, because they were firing at too long range."

Lapulapu's warriors, seeing that Magellan led the landing party, concentrated their fire on him. "But as a good captain and a knight," Pigafetta continued, "he still stood fast with some others, fighting thus for more than an hour. And as he refused to retire further, an Indian threw a bamboo lance in his face, and the captain immediately killed him with his lance, leaving it in his body. Then, trying to lay hand on his sword, he could draw it out but halfway, because of a wound from a bamboo lance that he had in his arm. Which seeing, all those people threw themselves on him, and one of them with a large javelin thrust it into his left leg, whereby he fell face downward. On this, all at once rushed upon him with lances of iron and of bamboo and with these javelins, so that they slew our mirror, our light, our comfort and our true guide."

The surviving members of the expedition were utterly devastated by their loss. They could not decide on who should succeed Magellan, which was understandable, for no one could replace him. The men finally voted on a joint command with the leadership divided between Duarte Barbosa and João Serrão, and shaped a course for Cebu and its friendly Rajah Humabon. But within four days the new leaders, too, were dead and the expedition was teetering on the brink of disaster.

Architect of this new calamity was Magellan's slave, Enrique, who had been promised his freedom in the event of his master's death. Barbosa roughly told him, wrote Pigafetta, that "although the captain his master was dead, he would not be set free or released, but that, when we reached Spain, he would still be the slave of Madame Beatriz, the wife of the deceased captain general."

Enrique thereupon stole ashore and, Pigafetta recounts, "told the Christian king that we were about to depart immediately, but that, if he would follow his advice, he would gain all our ships and merchandise. And so they plotted a conspiracy."

On May 1, Rajah Humabon, whose conversion to Christianity apparently was short-lived, invited the two new commanders to feast with him ashore. Serrão and Barbosa accepted the invitation, taking along 27 men, including one of the fleet's pilots, João Lopez Carvalho and the chief marshal, Gonzalo Gomez de Espinosa.

As the feast progressed, Carvalho and Espinosa uneasily became aware of a sinister atmosphere and returned, alone, to the ships. They had scarcely reached safety when an uproar broke out ashore. Carvalho took command, ordering the remaining crewmen to raise anchor and fire on Humabon's town. "Firing thus," Pigafetta recounted, "we perceived João Serrão bound and wounded, who cried out that we should not shoot any more for they would kill him. And we asked him if all the others were dead. And he said that all were dead save Enrique, and he begged us earnestly to redeem him with some merchandise. But João Carvalho, his friend, would not do so for fear that they would not remain masters if the boat were sent ashore. Then João Serrão, weeping, said that he prayed God that at the day of judgment he would demand his soul of his friend João Carvalho. Thereupon we departed quickly. And I know not whether João Serrão who remained behind be alive or dead."

The survivors of the Cebu massacre now followed Carvalho on a list-

less journey through the Philippine archipelago that lasted six months. They were months of blurred shadow; the surviving chronicles and logbooks with precise dates missing give a sense of aimless limbo. None of the men who eventually returned to Spain showed any willingness to explain their erratic odyssey. Under a more resolute leader than Carvalho they could have reached the Spice Islands in a fortnight.

Carvalho did have two exceedingly serious problems. One was a lack of manpower. More than 250 men had sailed from Spain; desertion, disease, accidents and the losses suffered in the Philippine battles had reduced the number to about 130, scarcely 40 men per ship, hardly enough to work them efficiently. Off the island of Bohol, therefore, the *Concepción* was stripped of all useful cargo and gear and then burned, and her crew was divided between the *Trinidad* and *Victoria*.

Carvalho's second problem could not be solved so easily: food. Any attempt to secure food from the islanders by force was unthinkable. If their precious trade goods were used up in bartering for supplies, there would be no point in reaching the Spice Islands at all. Somehow they must find an island where provisions were abundant.

After much fruitless wandering, while the food stocks dwindled to the vanishing point, the *Trinidad* and *Victoria* finally fetched up at the island of Palawan, which proved, in Pigafetta's words, a veritable "Land

Birds of paradise, expertly skinned so that their lustrous tawny-colored plumage was left intact, were among the gifts that the Moluccans showered on the Spaniards to take back to King Charles. The astounded explorers listened to legends that the birds came from heaven and flew constantly until they fell dead from the sky because they had no legs—which seemed true since Malay traders, who caught the birds in New Guinea, cut off the birds' legs before drying the skins.

of Promise.'' Here the islanders grew "rice, ginger, swine, goats, poultry, figs half a cubit long and as thick as the arm, which are good, and some others much smaller, which are better than all the others. There are also coconuts, sweet potatoes, sugar canes and roots like turnips.'' The explorers filled their holds and pushed on—to a disgraceful episode in which Carvalho enraged an island chieftan and disgusted his own men.

At Brunei, on the northwest coast of Borneo, the explorers were engaged in a lively trade with the townspeople when the lookouts were horrified to see the harbor filling with an armada of *praos*, fast lateen-rigged dugout canoes with outriggers. It was the local rajah's fleet returning from a foray against another potentate, and no harm was meant. But the jittery Carvalho believed an attack was imminent and decided to strike first. Abandoning five men who were trading ashore, he captured a large junk and took everyone aboard hostage, including three women. He then entered into some desultory negotiations with the rajah; when those were stalemated, he sailed away with his captives, leaving the men ashore to their fates—just as he had abandoned João Serrão on Cebu. Carvalho further disenchanted his crew by ransoming the male captives for gold he kept himself, and retaining the women as a private harem.

Sailing northward along the Borneo coast, Carvalho careened the sea-weary ships on an isolated island in the Balabac Strait and then at last took up a southeasterly course for the Moluccas.

Pigafetta described their arrival at these long-sought islands with justifiable emotion. They had picked up a local pilot by the simple expedient of capturing one on Sarangani Island in the southern Philippines. On November 6 they sighted some islands to the east, and the pilot identified them as the Moluccas. "Wherefore we gave thanks to God, and for our great joy we discharged all our artillery. It is no wonder that we should be so joyful, for we had suffered travail and perils for the space of twenty-five months less two days in the search for the Moluccas." Here they were at last, the Spice Islands—Ternate, Tidore, Bachan, Moti and Makian—the only places in the world where the clove tree grew. By good fortune the *Victoria* and *Trinidad* anchored off Tidore, whose Rajah Sultan El-Mansur welcomed them with delight. The Portuguese had supported the rival Sultan of Ternate in his feud with Tidore.

For once, the surviving officers and crewmen of the *Victoria* and *Trinidad* did nothing to alienate the island peoples. Instead they persuaded Carvalho to part with his harem and offer it as a gift to the Sultan of Tidore. That delighted worthy responded with a lavish supply of cloves and, as a going-away present, two stuffed birds of paradise with brilliantly colored plumage.

By December 18 the ships were ready to weigh anchor. Just then the *Trinidad* sprang a leak. "We heard the water entering as if through a pipe, but we could not find the place where it entered," reported Pigafetta. "All that day and the next we did nothing but work the pump, but all to no purpose." The Sultan sent to a neighboring town for some expert divers. Still the leak eluded detection. There was nothing for it but to unload the *Trinidad* and careen her on the beach.

Meanwhile, the *Victoria* had to sail for home. The seasonal easterly winds of the Indies had already begun to blow, and they would be

Shrewd, wary and proud, the Basque adventurer Juan Sebastián del Cano wears the air of a man who has been through conspiracy, starvation, tempest and sudden death, in this contemporary portrait. Though he plotted meanly against Magellan at one point, del Cano rose to greatness after the leader's death by taking command of the Victoria and sailing her safely home to Spain.

essential for a fast passage across the southern Indian Ocean to the Cape of Good Hope. Carvalho, Espinosa and 52 others chose to remain with the *Trinidad* and attempt to return back across the Pacific. Many of the men actually felt such a voyage was preferable to the course the *Victoria* would take, risking interception by hostile Portuguese all the way from the Moluccas to the Canaries. They accordingly made their plans cheerfully for the return trip—a trip that would prove full of surprises and disasters (pages 160-161). The remaining 47 men—plus 13 Moluccans who had agreed to sail to Spain and become interpreters—agreed to ship aboard the *Victoria,* whose captain was now Juan Sebastián del Cano, formerly master of the *Concepción.* Among them was the indefatigable Antonio Pigafetta.

Del Cano remains one of history's shadowy figures. He appears to have been born in 1486 or 1487 in northern Spain and to have gone to sea at an early age. He had captained a ship before signing on with Magellan's expedition. He took a minor part in the San Julian mutiny after the Atlantic crossing but was pardoned by Magellan. He had since proved himself an excellent seaman. After Magellan's death his stature grew as the men became disenchanted with Carvalho. By the time they reached the Moluccas, del Cano was regarded by many as a natural leader.

The *Victoria* hoisted sail on December 21, 1521, Moluccan pilots having been provided to guide del Cano out of the archipelago. Men from the *Trinidad* party came out from the shore in boats to say goodbye. Pigafetta found the moment of parting an emotional one: "The time being come, the ships took leave one of another by firing of guns," he recalled, "and it seemed that they were lamenting their last parting."

In del Cano's view, it was essential to make a swift and unobtrusive exit from the eastern fringe of the Indies, keeping well clear of the Portuguese trade route from Malacca to the Spice Islands. He therefore headed south, reaching the island of Ambon on December 29 and striking out across the Banda Sea, eventually arriving off the eastern tip of Timor on January 25, 1522. Next he steered southwest into the open ocean and set off on the hazardous voyage to the Cape of Good Hope.

Once again it was a race to reach a friendly landfall before the crew died of starvation or scurvy. But this time conditions were even worse than on that terrible voyage west across the Pacific. The men of the *Victoria* did not have fine weather and following winds but found themselves in an incessant battle against a west wind, constantly tacking to and fro in intense cold, with hunger and fatigue completing the deadly trinity. The men who survived looked back on the *Victoria's* homeward voyage as an unspeakable ordeal whose details were best forgotten. Pigafetta and the pilot, Albo, between them set down only the barest outline.

Del Cano started with a long run west-southwest to lat. 42° to get below the latitude of the cape. This, the easiest leg of the voyage, amounted to more than 3,500 miles across empty ocean—longer than the first Atlantic crossing with which Columbus had astonished Europe only 30 years before, and accomplished in the similar time of 36 days.

Then on March 22 del Cano began the westward haul to the cape and the agony of the *Victoria's* crew began in earnest. The ship was leaking and demanded exhausting work at the pumps. All the meat from the Indies had rotted in the casks, reducing the men to an enfeebling diet of rice and water. On this they lived for seven weeks as the *Victoria* lurched through heavy seas and adverse winds.

The vessel reached the cape at last and rounded it—only to have both her foremast and yard split by a storm. It was a particularly cruel setback. As the *Victoria* staggered into the South Atlantic on May 19, every fraction of speed was needed to reach land before the last of the rice ran out. But now, unable to carry sails on her foremast, she could only wallow along on main and mizzen, an ungainly cripple, reduced to a crawl. As the weeks dragged by with pitifully small daily runs to record, the fears of starvation became a terrible reality.

"We sailed northwest for two months continually without taking any refreshment or repose," wrote Pigafetta. "And in that short space of time twenty-one of our men died." Only a tireless chronicler such as Pigafetta would have troubled to remark that Moluccan corpses when flung overboard floated face downward while Christian corpses floated with their faces piously upturned to heaven.

Nursing along his crippled and leaking vessel, with scarcely more than 30 men able to lay a hand to rope, del Cano had no choice but to put

The fate of the forgotten "Trinidad"

The Trinidad's captured crew was forced by the Portuguese to build a fort (inset) on volcanic Ternate, romanticized in this Dutch engraving.

into the Portuguese-controlled Cape Verdes for food and water. He had a convincing story with which to allay Portuguese suspicions—the *Victoria* had been part of a Spanish fleet scattered by storms while coming home from Spanish America, as witness her ruined foremast.

Del Cano's bluff came within an ace of success. The Portuguese authorities accepted his story and agreed to provide food—but when a shore party of 13 men went to collect it, del Cano's cunning was undone by human stupidity. There are two versions of what happened, one being that a boastful crewman showed off his personal packet of cloves, the other that cloves were offered in lieu of money. In any case, the result was the same. Cloves in Spanish hands could have only one meaning: these were Magellan's men. The shore party was hauled off to jail after only two boatloads of rice had been ferried out to the *Victoria*. Del Cano answered the Portuguese governor's demand for surrender by heading straight out to sea. He was fortunate that there were no fast Portuguese men-of-war in the Cape Verdes, for the *Victoria* would never have been able to outpace them.

So they came home at last, a floating wreck with a handful of emaciated survivors and a cargo of cloves. "On Saturday the sixth of September, one thousand five hundred and twenty-two, we entered the Bay of San

Amid all the rejoicing at the *Victoria's* return from its circumnavigation, little concern was shown for the missing *Trinidad*. Yet what happened to her and her crew ranks among the great misadventures of exploration.

Aboard the *Trinidad* were 54 men, including Captain Gonzalo Gomez de Espinosa and veteran pilot João Lopez Carvalho. On December 18 they sailed from the Moluccas with the *Victoria*, westward for Africa and Spain. But scarcely had they weighed anchor than the *Trinidad* burst her seams, being packed with cloves beyond capacity—her first catastrophic misfortune.

After bidding farewell to the *Victoria*, the crew spent three grueling months repairing the *Trinidad*. Carvalho died of exhaustion. His loss was a disaster, for everyone was counting on him to navigate them home.

Winds were now unfavorable for a westward crossing, so instead the men planned to sail east to the Isthmus of Panama, where they could transship

the cloves to a vessel bound for Spain. But no sooner had they started than westerlies buffeted them north. For 15 weeks the *Trinidad* struggled to shape a course east but ended up off Japan.

The men were dying of hunger and unaccustomed cold when a vicious storm struck, tearing away the mainmast, the forecastle and poop. In despair, Espinosa turned back. For three and a half months the *Trinidad* wallowed south, men perishing by the dozen. When at last they reached the Moluccas, only 19 gaunt and popeyed wretches were alive—to discover in horror that a hostile Portuguese fleet was waiting for them.

Demoralized, the Spaniards surrendered, and then man's inhumanity to man replaced nature's wrath. When the *Trinidad* dragged her anchor in a squall and broke up on a reef, the Portuguese forced the prisoners to salvage her spars and build a fort that became their prison. From one island prison they were shipped to another and an-

other until they reached India. Some died in the stinking holds of prison ships; others succumbed to beatings and disease. Finally only Espinosa and five others remained alive.

With cunning born of desperation, three men escaped by ship from India. But to no avail—one died in the attempt, the other two were jailed upon reaching Lisbon. Eventually Espinosa and the remaining two were shipped in chains to Lisbon, where one died.

At last, the Portuguese were done with them. Three years after they had embarked on the *Trinidad's* last voyage, the four emaciated survivors were returned to Spain. In recognition of their ordeal, they were granted modest pensions by the King. But fate was not finished with the star-crossed Captain Espinosa. Trying to collect back pay, he was docked for the time he had been imprisoned. It was incontestable, the authorities ruled, that while a prisoner of the Portuguese, Espinosa was not in the service of Spain.

Lúcar, and we were only eighteen men, the most part sick, of the sixty remaining who had left Molucca. From the time when we departed from that bay until the present day," Pigafetta continued, "we had sailed fourteen thousand four hundred and sixty leagues, and completed the circuit of the world from east to west."

Two days later the *Victoria* anchored at Seville with a triumphant salute from her guns, and del Cano led all who could stagger on a barefoot procession to the shrines of Santa Maria de la Victoria and Santa Maria de la Antigua. They passed painfully through the streets, each survivor carrying a lighted candle, shocking the citizens of Seville with their gaunt and tormented appearance.

There was little profit from this tremendous venture. Charles sold the *Victoria*'s cargo of 26 tons of cloves for 10,000 times its cost of purchase, but this was barely enough for a small surplus after paying the costs of the voyage. The King awarded del Cano a modest pension and a coat of arms. This showed a globe with the proud Latin motto *Primus circumdedisti me*, "You were the first to circumnavigate me."

As for Doña Beatriz, Magellan's wife, she had died and so had the son she had borne him just before his departure. The returned crewmen were never paid in full since the voyage's profits had been so scanty; many were still suing for back pay years after their return home.

Apart from recovering the cost of the voyage, Spain derived little immediate benefit from the discoveries. The distances were too great for the dimunitive ships; they were unable to carry both trading goods and sufficient supplies. After a disastrous attempt at a second voyage in 1525, Charles decided to cut his losses in the Indies. In the Treaty of Saragossa, in 1529, Spain abandoned her claim to the Moluccas in return for 350,000 ducats, acceding to the contention that the islands lay within the Portuguese zone of influence. When the Spaniards continued their exploration of the Pacific later in the century, they did so from Panama.

Magellan's ghost can have found only two crumbs of comfort. His name was cleared by the inquiry ordered by Charles into the San Julian mutiny, and his excellent work in the Philippines did not go for nothing. The islands became Spain's biggest Pacific colony and remained so for more than three and a half centuries.

The true paradox of Magellan is that he was a man of action, seeking concrete results and hard profit, whose greatest achievement turned out to be the advancement of human knowledge. His voyage became a turning point in world history. In proving that ships could sail around the planet, Magellan ended a long era in which men had lived in a constantly expanding world. Other explorers would follow him; other discoveries would be made—but everything discovered on the face of the earth after Magellan's voyage would shrink the world instead of expanding it.

The work of the explorers did not go unrecognized in their own time. Within 20 years of Magellan's death the historian Gonzalo Fernández de Oviedo penned the following tribute: "The track the *Victoria* followed is the most wonderful thing and the greatest novelty that has ever been seen from the time God created the first man and ordered the world unto our own day. Neither has anything more notable in navigation ever been heard or described since the voyage of the patriarch Noah."

The Spice Islands of the East Indies are identified by name on this Spanish chart that was drawn in 1522, soon after Juan Sebastián del Cano's return from the circumnavigation. Naturally, Spanish cartographers interpreted the 1494 Treaty of Tordesillas dividing up the world so that the Moluccas and the Philippines fell well inside Spain's provenance and not Portugal's (vertical red line). Illustrations of fanciful cities bear names from Marco Polo's book, and various kings—of Persia, India, Bengal, China and Burma—are depicted in their royal trappings.

After discovery: the spoils of exploitation

None of the explorers—not Columbus, not da Gama, not Magellan—could possibly have imagined the epic forces their journeys would set in motion. Neither Columbus' discovery of the New World nor the circumnavigation by Magellan's crew returned much immediate profit to Spain. Yet within 50 years she was the world's richest nation, ruling an empire that comprised one third of the Western Hemisphere and spanned the Pacific west to the Philippines.

With brutal efficiency the conquistador Hernán Cortés sailed west from Cuba in 1519 to crush Mexico's Aztec civilization and grasp for Spain its immense wealth of gold and silver. With Mexico as a base, Spanish conquistadors swiftly subdued the peoples of central and western North America, and shipped the stolen lucre home. Striking south from Panama, Francisco Pizarro conquered the fabulously rich Peruvian Incas and paved the way for a thrust into Chile. Across the Pacific, one or two great galleons sailed each year from the Philippines loaded with precious cargoes of silk. By 1650 an awesome 181 tons of gold and 16,000 tons of silver had been taken from Spain's empire.

The Portuguese profited almost as handsomely—and even more quickly. The route da Gama pioneered around Africa to India was traveled by scores of Portuguese vessels by the time Magellan intruded on Spain's behalf. Portuguese colonies in India and the Moluccan Spice Islands provided a veritable cornucopia of riches. And the Portuguese felt their way farther and farther east, until by 1542 their traders had penetrated all the way to Japan.

During these years, Spain and Portugal proceeded as if by divine right—and, indeed, with papal approval. But in 1540 the French King, Francis I—with a theological impudence uncommon then—snapped: "I should like to see Adam's will wherein he divided the earth between Spain and Portugal." He added that the seas were open, and possession should depend on occupation. The English and Dutch agreed, and before the end of another century, those nations were to be vying fiercely for empire all across the globe.

Commanded by Hernán Cortés, Spanish cannon clear the beach at Veracruz as Spanish horsemen gallop ashore on the east coast of Mexico in 1519. In the upper left-hand corner of this anonymous painting depicting the arrival of the Spanish conquistadors, a delegation of befeathered Aztec Indians seeks to mollify the warlike strangers with lavish gifts of cloth and gold. However, the Spanish forces—made up of 400 soldiers with 15 horses and 16 cannon—ruthlessly slaughtered the Aztecs, thus establishing the pattern for conquest of the New World.

Zuñi Indians put up a futile resistance to the advancing Spanish troops of Francisco Vásquez de Coronado, who marched north from Mexico in 1540, penetrating as far as modern-day Dodge City, Kansas. This painting, done in Holland about 1545 by Jan Mostaert, is thought to be the earliest European representation of the Americas; it shows the mixture of fact and fancy with which the far-off Spanish possessions were viewed. The clifflike dwellings resemble those described in reports by Coronado's men. But the trees, sheep, cows and rabbits are just what a Dutch stay-at-home would see in his own barnyard.

168

Portuguese merchants, having reached the farthest ends of the Orient, disembark at a port in Japan. Though the Japanese caricatured the peculiar-looking Europeans with their long noses and baggy pants in works of art like this 16th Century screen painting, they received the traders with warmth, eagerly buying firearms for use in their own feudal warfare. They also welcomed missionaries, whom they saw as the companions of healthy trade; so effusive was the reception, in fact, that the first Jesuits to arrive in 1549 to proselytize among the Japanese delivered 2,000 converts to Christianity in the first two years.

The heyday of the Portuguese empire in the East Indies nears its end in 1639 as ships flying the red-white-and-blue-striped flag of the Netherlands direct a blast of cannon at a Portuguese merchant fleet anchored in the harbor at Goa, the principal city of Portugal's colonial empire for more than a century. The Dutch—champions of the Protestant Reformation and therefore no respecters of papal bulls—began as early as 1595 to encroach on Portuguese preserves on the eastern sea route; not long after the scene depicted in this 17th Century oil painting, much of the trade in the Indian Ocean was in the hands of the Dutch.

Bibliography

Axelson, Eric, *Congo to Cape*. Harper & Row, 1973.

Bry, Theodore de, *Discovering the New World*. Edited by Michael Alexander, Harper & Row, 1976.

Cameron, Ian, *Magellan And the First Circumnavigators of the World*. Saturday Review Press, 1973.

Casson, Lionel, *The Ancient Mariners: Seafarers and Sea Fighters of the Mediterranean in Ancient Times*. Macmillan, 1959.

Columbus, Ferdinando, *The Life of Admiral Christopher Columbus (by His Son Ferdinand)*. Translated and annotated by Benjamin Keen, Rutgers University Press, 1959.

Correa, Gaspar, *The Three Voyages of Vasco da Gama and His Viceroyalty*. Hakluyt Society, 1869.

Crone, G. R., *The Discovery of America: Atlantic Voyages of the Portuguese*. Hamish Hamilton, 1969.

Curtis, William Eleroy, *Christopher Columbus, His Portraits and Monuments*. 1893.

Fernández-Armesto, Felipe:
Columbus and the Conquest of the Impossible. Weidenfeld and Nicolson, 1974.
Ferdinand and Isabella. Weidenfeld and Nicolson, 1975.

Greenlee, William Brooks, *The Voyage of Pedro Alvares Cabral to Brazil and India*. Hakluyt Society, 1938.

Guillemard, F. H. H., *The Life of Ferdinand Magellan*. AMS Press, 1971.

Jayne, K. G., *Vasco da Gama and His Successors, 1460-1580*. Methuen, 1910.

Landström, Björn, *The Ship, An Illustrated History*. Doubleday, 1961.

Ley, Charles David, ed., *Portuguese Voyages 1498-1663*. E. P. Dutton, 1947.

McKendrick, Melveena, *Ferdinand and Isabella*. American Heritage, 1968.

Madariaga, Salvador de, *Christopher Columbus*. Frederick Ungar, 1967.

Martinez-Hidalgo, Jose Maria, *Columbus' Ships*. Barre Publishers, 1966.

Morison, Samuel Eliot:
Admiral of the Ocean Sea: A Life of Christopher Columbus. Little, Brown, 1942.
The European Discovery of America: The Southern Voyages, 1492-1616. Oxford University Press, 1974.
Ed. and trans., *Journals and Other Documents on the Life and Voyages of Christopher Columbus*. Heritage Press, 1963.

Moule, A. C., and Paul Pelliot, *Marco Polo The Description of the World*. Geo. Routledge, 1976.

Nowell, Charles E., *Magellan's Voyage Around the World*. Northwestern University Press, 1962.

Parr, Charles McKew, *So Noble A Captain: The Life and Times of Ferdinand Magellan*. Thomas Y. Crowell, 1953.

Parry, J. H.:
The Age of Reconnaissance. World, 1963.
The Discovery of the Sea. Dial Press, 1974.
The European Reconnaissance, Selected Documents. Walker, 1968.

Penrose, Boies, *Travel and Discovery in the Renaissance*. Harvard University Press, 1955.

Pigafetta, Antonio, *Magellan's Voyage*. Translated by R. A. Skelton, Yale University Press, 1969.

Ravenstein, E. G., *A Journal of the First Voyage of Vasco da Gama, 1497-1499*. Hakluyt Society, 1898.

Roditi, Edouard, *Magellan of the Pacific*. McGraw-Hill, 1972.

Sanceau, Elaine, *Henry the Navigator*. W. W. Norton, 1947.

Silverberg, Robert, *The Realm of Prester John*. Doubleday, 1972.

Skelton, R. A., *Explorers' Maps*. Spring Books, 1958.

Sykes, Sir Percy, *A History of Exploration*. Routledge & Kegan Paul, 1949.

Taylor, E. G. R., *The Haven-Finding Art*. American Elsevier Publishing, 1971.

Ure, John, *Prince Henry the Navigator*. Constable, 1977.

Zurara, Gomes Eannes de, *The Chronicle of the Discovery and Conquest of Guinea*, 2 vols. Translated by Charles Raymond Beazley and Edgar Prestage, Burt Franklin, 1963.

Picture Credits

Lisbon. 90: Estúdio M. Novais, courtesy Sociedade de Geografia, Lisbon. 93: Radio Times Hulton Picture Library, London—National Maritime Museum, London. 94: Istituto e Museo di Storia della Scienza, Florence—Derek Bayes, courtesy National Maritime Museum, London. 95: Rare Book Division, The New York Public Library, Astor, Lenox and Tilden Foundations; Derek Bayes, courtesy National Maritime Museum, London (2). 96: Estúdio M. Novais, courtesy Academia das Ciências, Lisbon; Derek Bayes, courtesy National Maritime Museum, London; Istituto e Museo di Storia della Scienza, Florence. 100, 101: Library of Congress. 102: A. Santos D'Almeida, courtesy Academia das Ciências, Lisbon. 103: Estúdio M. Novais, courtesy Museu de Marinha, Lisbon. 104, 105: Pierpont Morgan Library. 106, 107: By permission of the British Library. 108 through 117: Marcello Vivarelli, courtesy Biblioteca Casanatense, Rome. 118: Augusto Meneses, courtesy Museo Naval, Seville. 120: The Mansell Collection, London. 122: Aldo Durazzi, courtesy Galleria Borghese, Rome. 124, 125: Archivo General de Indias, Seville. 126, 127: Augusto Meneses, courtesy Museo de América, Madrid. 129: Augusto Meneses, courtesy Reales Alcázares, Seville. 130, 131: Photo Bibliothèque Nationale, Paris. 132: Library of Congress. 134, 135: Library of Congress—Photo Bulloz, Paris. 136 through 145: Drawings by Richard Schlecht. 146: Reghis Romero III. 150, 151: The Newberry Library by permission of Professor Charles R. Boxer. 152: David Lees, courtesy Museo Civico, Vicenza; Photo Bibliothèque Nationale, Paris. 153: Photo Bibliothèque Nationale, Paris. 154, 157: Library of Congress. 159: Augusto Meneses, courtesy Museo Naval, Seville. 160: Library of Congress. 163: Chomon-Perino, courtesy Biblioteca Reale, Turin. 164, 165: Reproduced by courtesy of the owner Miss M. L. A. Strickland and the Department of the Environment, London, copyright Aldus Books. 166, 167: Scala, courtesy State-Owned Art Collections Department, The Hague, on loan to the Frans Halsmuseum, Haarlem. 168, 169: Michael Holford Library, London, courtesy Musée Guimet, Paris. 170, 171: Rijksmuseum, Amsterdam.

Acknowledgments

The index for this book was prepared by Anita R. Beckerman.

The editors wish to thank the following artists: John Batchelor (pages 44-51, 70-71), Peter McGinn (end-paper maps) and Richard Schlecht (pages 136-145). The editors also wish to thank: In Lisbon: Teixeira da Mota, Secretary General, Academia das Ciencias; Jose Pereira da Costa, Director, Arquivo Nacional; Library and Museum Staff, Museu da Marinha; Antonio de Almeida, Secretary; Alexandre Marques Pereira, Librarian, Library and Museum Staff, Sociedade de Geografia. In London: J. M. Backhouse, Assistant Keeper, H. M. T. Cobbe, Assistant Keeper, Mark Evans, Research Assistant, D. H. Turner, Deputy Keeper, Department of Western Manuscripts; John Huddy, Map Room; B. Hutchinson, Department of Medieval and Later Antiquities; Norah Titley, Department of Oriental Manuscripts; British Library; M. D. McLeod, Keeper, J. W. Picton, Deputy Keeper, Department of Ethnography; R. Williams, Department of Prints and Drawings; British Museum; E. H. H. Archibald, Curator of Oil Paintings; David Lyon, Stephen Reilly, Department of Ships; Joan Moore, Photographic Services; C. J. Mortar, Carol Stott, Department of Navigation and Astronomy; Roger Quarm, Department of Prints and Drawings; National Maritime Museum; Dr. L. Hallewell, Assistant Librarian, School of Oriental and African Studies. Also in England: R. C. Latham, Pepys Library, Magdalene College, Cambridge; W. O. Hassall, C. Starks, Department of Western Manuscripts, Bodleian Library, Oxford. In Madrid: Garcia Cubera, Biblioteca National; Don Fermin Munoz, Secretario, Casa de Alba; Ibanez Cerda, Instituto de Cultura Hispanica; Don Cristobal Colon, Duque de Veragua, Ministerio de la Marina; Padre Teodoro Alonso, Bibliotecario, Monasterio del Escorial; General José Angosto Gomez Castrillon, Director, Museo del Ejercito; José Maria Zumacalarregui, Director, Museo Naval; Fernando Fuertes de Villaviciencio, Consejero Delegado Gerente, Real Patrimonio. Also in Spain: Doña Rosario Parra, Director, Archivo de las Indias; Francisco Alvarez Seisdedos, Director, Biblioteca Colombina; Don Rafael Manzano, Director, Real Alcazar, Seville; Amando Represa, Director, Archivo de Simancas, Valladolid. In Paris: Lucie Lagarde, Curator; Monique de la Roncière, Curator, Département des Cartes et Plans, Bibliothèque Nationale; Denise Chaussegroux, Researcher; Hervé Cras, Director for Documentary Studies, Musée de la Marine. In New York: Kenneth Lohf, Librarian, Rare Books and Manuscripts, Columbia University; Priscilla Muller, Curator of the Museum, Hispanic Society of America; Rare Book Division, The New York Public Library; Evelyn Semler, The Pierpont Morgan Library. In Washington, D.C.: Map Division, Library of Congress; Louis Vigneras, The Folger Shakespeare Library; George C. Watson, Curator, Department of Vertebrate Zoology, Smithsonian Institution. The editors also wish to thank: Professor Eric Axelson, Assistant Principal, University of Cape Town, Rondebosch, South Africa.

Quotations from Antonio Pigafetta's Magellan's Voyage, translated and edited by R. A. Skelton, © 1969, reproduced by permission of Yale University Press. Other particularly valuable sources for this book were: Journals and Other Documents on the Life and Voyages of Christopher Columbus, edited and translated by Samuel Eliot Morison, Heritage Press, 1963 and Mr. Morison's Admiral of the Ocean Sea, Little, Brown, 1942; also The Chronicle of the Discovery and Conquest of Guinea by Gomes Eannes de Zurara, translated by Charles Raymond Beazley and Edgar Prestage, Burt Franklin, 1963.

Index

Printed in U.S.A.

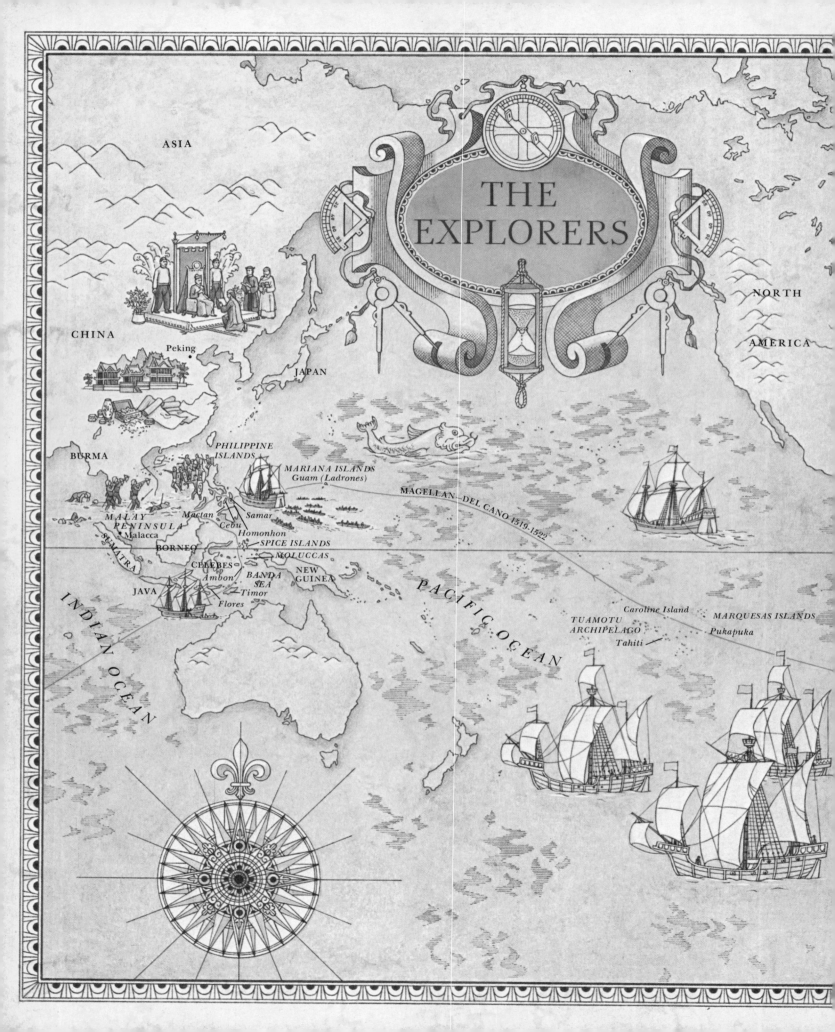

THE EXPLORERS

ASIA

NORTH

AMERICA

CHINA

Peking

JAPAN

BURMA

PHILIPPINE
ISLANDS

MARIANA ISLANDS
Guam (Ladrones)

MAGELLAN - DEL CANO 1519-1522

MALAY
PENINSULA

Mactan

Samar

Malacca

Cebu

SUMATRA

Homonhon

BORNEO

SPICE ISLANDS

MOLUCCAS

CELEBES

Ambon

BANDA
SEA

NEW
GUINEA

PACIFIC OCEAN

JAVA

Timor

Flores

INDIAN OCEAN

Caroline Island

MARQUESAS ISLANDS

TUAMOTU
ARCHIPELAGO

Pukapuka

Tahiti